Best Signature Outdoor Kitchens

CREATIVE HOMEOWNER®, Upper Saddle River, New Jersey

First published in book form in 2012 by

CREATIVE
HOMEOWNER®

A Division of Federal Marketing Corp.
Upper Saddle River, NJ

Signature Kitchens & Baths Magazine is published by Magnolia Media Group

VICE PRESIDENT & PUBLISHER	Timothy O. Bakke
MANAGING EDITOR	Fran J. Donegan
ART DIRECTOR	David Geer
SENIOR EDITOR	Kathie Robitz
PRODUCTION COORDINATOR	Sara M. Markowitz
COVER	Rachele Juliano, Kathy Wityk
LAYOUT	Rachele Juliano, Kathy Wityk
DIGITAL IMAGING SPECIALIST	Mary Dolan
FRONT COVER PHOTOGRAPH	Andrea Bricco
BACK COVER	(top left) Matt Chadwick; (top right) Andrea Bricco; (bottom left) courtesy of KitchenAid; (bottom right) courtesy of Viking Range

Manufactured in the United States of America

Current Printing (last digit)
10 9 8 7 6 5 4 3 2 1

Best Signature Outdoor Kitchens
Library of Congress Control Number: 2011925583
ISBN-10: 1-58011-531-4
ISBN-13: 978-1-58011-531-5

CREATIVE HOMEOWNER®
A Division of Federal Marketing Corp.
24 Park Way
Upper Saddle River, NJ 07458
www.creativehomeowner.com

CONTENTS

SOME BASICS

THE KITCHENS

Outdoor Fare

Turn your outdoor space into an epicurean paradise with these fantastic ideas.

By Alison Rich

In years past, dining outside meant firing up the grill, slapping on some burgers and dogs, sitting at the traditional table-and-bench setup, and calling it a day. All prep work took place inside, with the chef busily schlepping grub and other goodies to and from the house. But that arrangement is quickly going out the window as boundaries continue to blur between the interior and exterior living spaces, and homeowners discover the convenience of an outdoor kitchen.

The outdoor kitchen may be part of a larger outdoor area, such as this space by Fire Stone Home Products.

"People are bringing their entertaining more and more to the outside," said Kevin Cunningham, president of Geneva, Illinois-based Ultimate Outdoor Kitchens. "They want to stay outside and make that area an outdoor room, just like you would a living room. And they want to set it up with TVs, stereos, and all of the conveniences they have inside." And thanks to the extensive selection of outdoor kitchen products on the market today, crafting a pleasing design that meets your needs—while meeting with nature—is a bona-fide breeze.

THE ESSENTIAL INGREDIENTS Typically, an outdoor kitchen includes a grill, a side burner, a sink, a refrigerator, and maybe a warming drawer, says Michael Logsdon, president of Boerne, Texas-based Land Design. "Those are the basics." And from there, you can add bells and whistles, which include such frills

as outdoor dishwashers, microwaves, ice makers, beer taps, wine coolers, sinks, margarita machines, and even small appliances such as blenders—in short, stuff that used to be relegated to the indoors is now available for use outdoors.

When fashioning an outdoor kitchen, the first thing Lodgson does is interview the client to ascertain their price point and desires and to ensure the design will be useful for them. "It's part of programming the design, and each client is different," he said. He asks whether the client has children, entertains often and, if so, how many visitors they typically host. "It's building the program for their specific wants, needs, lifestyle, and budget," he explains.

LAY OF THE LAND When it comes to the layout, Logsdon adheres to the "classic work triangle" approach, an efficient arrangement that keeps everything close at hand. For example, the fridge, the grill, and the sink are all within a few steps from each other. "It's the same theory as laying out a kitchen in the house," he said of the work-triangle approach. "It's making things accessible in the fewest steps," he said, "with places to set things when you're cooking so that you can get to them easily." Minimizing the amount of time spent traveling from spot to spot makes it much simpler to make quick work of the tasks at hand. "If you can take one or two steps," he said, "it's better than five or six."

As most of us know all too well, wind can wreak havoc on outdoor activities, so it's prudent to consider its direction when creating a user-friendly cooking zone, Cunningham advises. "If the wind's whipping around, it may go through the back of the grill and blow out the burners," he said. After he studies the patio layout, Cunningham then positions the desired appliances at optimal angles to mitigate potential weather-related snafus.

Another thought: does the chef need drawers for utensils? And is the client right- or left-handed? "It makes a difference where you grab your utensils," he noted. But, essentially, Cunningham, like Logsdon, adheres to the same precepts for creating an outdoor kitchen as he does when designing one for inside the house.

BEAUTY ON THE OUTSIDE As with most things in life, beauty is in the eye of the beholder, and outside spaces are no exception, Cunningham says. "It all depends on their take on comfort. How do they want to lay it out? Is there a pool? How many people do they entertain? Do they want a roof or

A kitchen island with integrated appliances keeps everything within reach, an important design consideration of your outdoor kitchen.

pergola over it because of the sun?" he said. "It's based on what they want and their idea of comfort." One of his clients actually installed radiant heaters in his outdoor kitchen to extend its usefulness throughout the entire year. While some might balk at outdoor cooking when the mercury dips, others jump at the chance—a definite case in point for the subjective nature of comfort and why establishing rapport with clients is so important to designers.

As far as comfort is concerned, it's linked to the layout, Logsdon says. He is keen on using fireplace hearths for passive seating as well as chairs with ottomans and squishy cushions—elements that add comfort. "It's like laying out a kitchen and a living room. I bring in some living room-type things so while you're cooking, people can lounge around and be comfortable," he said, likening his style to traditional country kitchens that exude a welcoming air. "That's how I do outdoor kitchens. It's sort of a living room/kitchen/family room."

The yin-and-yang combo of fire and water is also a winning mix, Logsdon says, and a cool way to evoke comfort in an outdoor kitchen, he notes. "That's why we do pools and fire features." Fireplaces and fire pits inject an air of welcoming warmth and help make a "comfortable, efficient, user-friendly kitchen," he added.

Will the trend continue? Cunningham thinks so. "It's becoming bigger and bigger," he said." I think people want to stay home and entertain at the house."

And with the abundance of outdoor-living options from which to choose, there's no doubt they'll have tons of fun doing it!

OUTWARD BOUND

Outfit your backyard kitchen with these outdoor appliances,
an outcropping of all-weather wonders guaranteed to ensure
that your outer space is right on cue.

// By Haley Owens and Alison Rich

Party-Ready Patio // Gussy up your grill zone with KitchenAid's Outdoor Kitchen Line. The complete collection includes 27-, 36-, and 48-in. built-in grills; refrigerator; ice makers and serving cart; and built-in warming, trash, and utility drawers; along with freestanding and built-in refreshment centers. This appliance grouping also features electric warming drawers, built-in thermometers, and interior halogen lights (on built-in models). KitchenAid, www.kitchenaid.com.

Works Like Magic // This RH Peterson Fire Magic side burner (left) is oversized and specially designed to accommodate large skillets and woks. Pair it with a Fire Magic grill for the ultimate open-air kitchen and outdoor entertainment center. RH Peterson Fire Magic, www.rhpeterson.com.

Upper Crusts // No matter how you slice it, Kalamazoo's Outdoor Gourmet Artisan Fire Pizza Oven (right) is a delicious addition to your outdoor appliances. The first countertop oven with two independently controlled burners, it lets you bake any type of pie, as well as calzones and artisanal breads. One burner warms the baking stone, while the other heats the interior and browns toppings to ooey-gooey greatness. Now that's our kind of delivery service! Kalamazoo Outdoor Gourmet, www.kalamazoogourmet.com.

Task Master // DCS by Fisher & Paykel's Outdoor Module System (above) combines a standard outdoor kitchen setup with the versatile 360-deg. grilling of the Liberty Collection. This versatile appliance comes complete with a cache of professionally styled 30-in. cooking components: the All-Grill, the Side-Burner Sink, and the Side-Burner Griddle. DCS by Fisher & Paykel, www.fisherpaykel.com.

Exterior Motives // You can have every culinary amenity under the sun with this fully loaded suite of Viking outdoor appliances. Whether the recipe calls for grilling, smoking, stir-frying, cooking on a rotisserie, or baking, you'll be set for success. Warming drawers keep your foods toasty after they come off the fire. Refrigerated storage and dispensers seal in the cool, and stainless-steel cabinets corral all your outer wares in one easy-to-access module. Viking, www.vikingrange.com.

Warming Trends // Even when the weather report is iffy, the temperature of your food always will be right on the money, thanks to the VEWD warming drawer by Viking. The flexible moisture control and temperature settings —from 90 to 250 deg. F.—keep plated meals toasty without drying them out, serve up steamy soups and stews, and proof a loaf of bread before popping it in the oven. The warming drawer is available in stainless steel with an optional brass trim. Viking, www.vikingrange.com.

Think Drinks // It may be compact, but U-Line's Outdoor Series Refrigerator (left) is big on convenience and huge on cool. The Touch Glass digital temperature keeps food and beverages cool in the warmest weather. The robust Pro Handle and fully wrapped stainless-steel door and cabinet prevent against wear-and-tear. Plus the perfectly proportioned 3-cu.-ft. interior grants space for a full stock of drinks and other tasty treats. U-Line, www.u-line.com.

Able Table // The Cook-N-Dine table (right) is an outdoor cooking center and dining table in one. Made of food-grade stainless steel, the hot cooking center lowers slightly to form a shallow pit while the outer eating area stays comfortably cool to the touch. And even though food is in direct contact with the heat source, no heat or energy loss occurs. When it's turned off, the cook surface reverts to flat, making it even with the rest of the table. No gas, charcoal, or any other fuel is needed—just a grounded power outlet. Cook-N-Dine, www.cook-n-dine-usa.com.

Frost Bites // Protect your perishables from heat with Sub-Zero's Outdoor Undercounter All Refrigerator (below). Sporting clean lines and a classic stainless-steel finish, its subdued silhouette complements outdoor kitchens of all shapes and sizes. And this nifty fridge's accessibility means you'll always have the noshes an cold drinks you need at hand. Sub-Zero, www.subzero.com.

Rack and Roll // The days of carting dishes and glasses inside for washing are of the past, thanks to Kalamazoo Outdoor Gourmet's first-ever outdoor dishwasher (above). Incorporating an innovative wash system, this appliance is designed to clean dishes that have been outside in the sun, and even pots and pans that have been sitting on the grill. It's easy to operate product and scrubs your kitchen wares to a clean sheen. Finally, an all-weather dishwasher that does the work for you! Kalamazoo Outdoor Gourmet, www.kalamazoogourmet.com.

Versatile VIP // Move out of the way, Bobby Flay. There's another celebrity chef in town … and it's you! With this outdoor appliance suite by Viking, you'll be cooking and creating under the sun and stars. The full spectrum of weather-ready products is guaranteed to put the sizzle in your steaks and in your soirees. Viking, www.vikingrange.com.

Grills of Your Dreams // You'll find everything you ever wanted for your outdoor kitchen with the Lynx Professional Grills family of products (below). From refrigerators to warming drawers to cocktail stations, patio heaters, ventilation, and more, the company manufactures it all. Each of the professional appliances merge proprietary technology with refined features. Lynx Professional Grills, www.lynxgrills.com.

Fire Power // Dacor's professional grills are designed for a custom built-in installation or as a freestanding grill on a stainless-steel cart (left). The company's newly launched Epicure line features five-star stylings and pro-level performance. Other features include: side burners; Illumina controls; easy-to-clean removable grease tray; built-in halogen lights; Perma-Flame instant reignition, removable rotisserie motor and fork set; V-shaped Even-Heat channels; removable smoker tray; and a spot-on temperature gauge. Dacor, www.dacor.com.

Top of Its Class // Designed to provide equal measures of beauty and efficiency, Danver's durable 32-in.-deep outdoor grill (left) provides exceptional capture area. It is available in 36-, 48-, and 60-in. widths. A powerful pair of internal sealed motors have a combined ventilation rating of 12.66 cu. ft. per minute (CFM). Stainless-steel commercial-grade baffle filters are also dishwasher safe. Dimmable 50-watt halogen lights illuminate the cooking area. Danver. www.danver.com

Well-Done Design // Evocative of Wolf's high quality indoor kitchen appliances, their double-wall stainless-steel grills, available in 30-, 36-, 42-, and 54-in. sizes are built to withstand the weather. This 36-in. model (right) is available as a built-in unit or on a freestanding cart. The side burner is optional. Wolf, www.wolfappliances.com.

PARTY-WORTHY PATIOS

These fabulous designs are idyllic places for entertaining guests in style.

// *By Heather Hill Cernoch*

AN INEVITABLE THING happens when the weather begins to warm. We instantly crave sunny spots outdoors with balmy breezes, comfy chairs, and perhaps a cool drink in hand. Some people imagine an oceanfront resort or an exotic locale, but these homeowners simply fling open their back doors to reveal glamorous outdoor living spaces.

For designer Sandra Espinet, these outdoor rooms are extensions of the indoors, where parties effortlessly spill out onto verandas and patios that blend naturally into the home's surroundings.

"I like starting with the natural elements of the location," Espinet says. "In Montana, we would design a very different outdoor setting, taking advantage of the mountain views, and in Cabo, we take advantage of the ocean views."

Even if your home is nowhere near a dramatic

landscape, it's possible to create an inviting outdoor environment for entertaining alfresco.

Natural Flow and Comfort // When designing an outdoor space, remember to create a natural flow between the interior and exterior living spaces.

"The easiest way to blend indoor and outdoor spaces is to use the same flooring and paint colors so that the two spaces are connected," Espinet says. "This way once you open up your sliding doors or pocket doors, it all becomes one big space."

Espinet also recommends cabana-style outdoor curtains that open onto a patio, creating the illusion that it's part of the inside. "With today's wonderful outdoor fabric selections, it is easy to do this," she says.

Treating the outdoor living area as an extension of the indoors will also ensure guest comfort.

"Making an outdoor space as comfortable as possible means accessorizing it and adding special touches as you would in your living room," Espinet says. "You just have to select items that are a bit more durable and weatherproof. I love outdoor dining "rooms" with chandeliers. They become full rooms without walls that truly integrate the inside and outside seamlessly."

But the most important consideration is adequate seating that's oriented "so guests always have a pretty view," she adds.

Outdoor Kitchen Essentials // "I love having the space and luxury of an outside bar and kitchen," Espinet says. "When we can build a separate pavilion for food activities and outdoor eating, we always put as much as we can outside—grill, pizza oven, sink, refrigerator, ice machine, and even wine coolers."

When incorporating a full kitchen into an outdoor entertainment area, first consider the amount of space you have and the kind of maintenance you're willing to do.

"The amount of maintenance required is usually part of the equation as more and more people are putting in larger outdoor living spaces that incorporate a kitchen, and they want no maintenance," says Mitch Slater of Danver, a manufacturer of stainless-steel cabinetry. "Some consideration has to be given to locations near saltwater, which increases the potential for more maintenance."

According to Slater, outdoor kitchen essentials include a food prep area, a cooking area, a holding zone with a warming drawer, a serving area with adjacent seating, and perhaps a bar.

"We are seeing more of a best-in-class selection of products that allow homeowners to do any kind of cooking they want [outside]," Slater says. "This usually means mixing manufacturers to obtain wood-fired pizza ovens, power burners for boils (lobsters, crabs, shrimp, crawfish, and stews), infrared grills for direct-heat cooking, charcoal 'eggs' for smoking and indirect-heat cooking, warming drawers, and the like. Given that they are mixing manufacturers' products, consistency in the cabinetry aids in making the look of the kitchen work."

Stainless-steel cabinetry, which Slater recommends for its durability, is customizable based on a kitchen's color scheme. Powder-coated finishes create signature looks, while the sturdiness of the stainless steel remains intact.

At least one manufacturer offers a multitude of colors as well as a realistic wood look in 10 different wood species.

"This goes a long way toward the demands of the homeowner because these painted surfaces are virtually maintenance free," Slater says. "A clear coat will retain the stainless look near the ocean without having to worry about maintenance to remove salt and keep the surface from having rust or pitting."

Got It Covered // Another consideration is whether to cover the outdoor kitchen and adjacent gathering area.

"The kitchen usually has a serving area facing the gathering space, which can be covered overhead or open," Slater says. "Our experience is that they tend to be open more in the Northeast and upper Midwest and covered in the hotter South, Southwest, and West."

A covered kitchen requires ventilation to remove smoke and grease fumes. According to Slater, most manufacturers' hoods are 27 inches deep, which isn't deep enough to capture smoke outside when the hood is mounted to the wall.

"I went to a domestic hood manufacturer and had him design a hood 32 inches deep, so it can mount directly to the wall," Slater says. "Homeowners usually know nothing of this and, in most cases, don't even think of ventilation until smoke builds up under their roof."

In addition, pizza ovens, a popular item in larger outdoor kitchens, give off a lot of heat. "It is usually better to keep [pizza ovens] some distance from the gathering area and kitchen zone so as not to overpower them with heat," Slater warns. "Keep this in mind when building a covered outdoor kitchen."

He notes that homeowners should also remember the small details that can add comfort and convenience to outdoor kitchens and entertaining areas, including patio heaters, perimeter insect control systems, and extra trash receptacles.

"I am building my own [outdoor kitchen] now, and I have a trash [receptacle] near the cooking area, one near the food prep, and another near the bar area," Slater says.

Smaller Spaces // In smaller spaces where full-size kitchens would be overwhelming, keep the design simple.

A "barbecue island," which is a popular alternative to an outdoor kitchen, is a one-piece, built-in-place or modular unit with cutouts for a grill, a side burner, and perhaps a refrigerator, Slater explains. Sometimes these islands include small drawers or a built-in trash receptacle, but they provide much less organization than a full kitchen.

When it doubt, consult a professional who can recommend an arrangement that's right for the space.

"Outdoor areas do not always have to have [full-size] kitchens," Espinet says. "But you always have to have comfortable lounging furniture. If you have limited space, I think it's best not to overcrowd the space and choose one type of outdoor furniture—such as chaise lounges or a built-in seating area."

Factoring in Functionality // For Espinet, the ideal space for outdoor entertaining includes several zones for various activities. If you have the room, establishing distinct areas keeps outdoor living versatile.

"You have to think about how a space will be used and what activities the homeowner will do in the outdoor spaces," Espinet says. "Lounging areas where you can read, relax,

or have a cocktail are great. And of course hammocks and unique seating such as the swivel canopy Orbit chair are always winners."

Espinet is also a proponent of adding a bit of a spark to outdoor settings. "You can have a lot of fun with guests by adding outdoor fire pits where everyone can have a drink after dinner or watch sunsets," she says.

"You can also dazzle guests with moonscape night lighting." To do this, direct exterior lights down from several points in a tree. "It looks as though light is coming from the moon," she adds.

For Slater, the popularity of outdoor entertaining areas paints a picture of the world we currently live in, where homeowners desire an attractive space for hosting gatherings that takes advantage of the great outdoors. It's a bigger notion than an outdoor cookout.

"I liken it to the concept of the indoor kitchen as the 'heart of the home,' he says. "This is the heart of the home outdoors. With the advent of more and more products to furnish the outdoor room, the kitchen is just one part of the space."«

Outdoor Design Tips | *from* **Sandra Espinet**

» Design your outdoor living area so that it's not wasted space. If you equip your patio properly, your family will use it.

» Go the extra mile to include finishing touches such as embroidered logo towels, towel hampers, pool floats, tilting umbrellas, and chaise lounges with wheels that can be moved with the sun.

» Outdoor tables should have their own plates, silverware, and linens so that no one worries about the more formal interior dishes.

» Shells and hurricane lamps with sand on the bottom are great weatherproof decor for an outdoor sitting area.

» If you have kids, incorporate a space they will enjoy.

paving the way

THE PRACTICAL AND PRETTY PRIMER OF A PERFECTLY PAVED HARDSCAPE LAYS THE GROUNDWORK FOR THE MOST ROCKIN' OUTDOOR DESIGNS. **BY HALEY OWENS**

PHOTOS PROVIDED BY BELGARD® HARDSCAPES.

CONSIDER THE LAST stunning under-the-sun setup you saw. Perhaps it had a well-appointed patio for gathering with guests, paved pathways for strolling through a lush garden, stone steps for ascending or descending to varying lawn levels, a pool deck for lounging waterside, or even a custom kitchen for firing up the grill. Chances are, as you admired the scenery, you complimented the lovely landscaping.

While this was likely at least partially true when considering the appeal, landscaping often gets all the glory due to its frequent use as a catchall term for an overall outdoor setting. However, despite its little recognition, it is actually hardscaping that often has the biggest impact in a backyard.

By serving as an extension of the home's architecture, creating functional walkways and bases for cooking and living areas, adding texture to the terrain, and more, hardscaping paves the way for both fun and functional outdoor design details. Here we lay the groundwork for how you can incorporate hardscaping into your own open-air rooms.

PRETTY PATIOS Even the smallest of yards may have a porch or patio, or the simplest concrete slab. But you can add a custom look by using pavers. With varying materials, colors, and textures—not to mention the plethora of pattern options—pavers are a finishing flourish that also offer unmatched durability and crack resistance. And as the size of the patio expands, so do the possibilities. Pavers come in a variety of sizes and shapes, and by artfully mixing materials, you can visually connect the hardscape to the home, draw discernible lines from the home into the landscape, and designate distinct areas.

LEADING THE WAY The idea that it's not the destination but the journey that counts couldn't ring truer than it does with beautifully hardscaped walkways. Even when not leading to any one spot in particular, paved paths can add visual interest and allow you to explore a landscape by bordering flowerbeds, crossing the yard, or rounding the house. For more purposeful walkways, imagine the overall design on a grid, and locate areas of interest off major axis points from the starting point, which would be the house or outdoor living area adjacent to the house.

TURNING UP THE HEAT Hardscapes encompass more than just stone-laid surfaces underfoot. They offer the opportunity to build up almost any amenity to create the atmosphere and ambiance desired. To add the festivity of alfresco dining with family and friends, built-in outdoor cooking quarters sizzle so much more than a stand-alone grill. But outdoor kitchens aren't the only trend heating up hardscapes. Fire features—from classic fireplaces that can serve as focal points to dramatic fire pits—add physical warmth on cool nights and a welcoming feeling year-round.

DECKING OUT WATERWAYS Cooling counterparts to fire features, swimming pools, fountains, and other water features often take center stage in the outdoor entertainment scene. In a supporting role, pavers play an important part in highlighting the designs. With the flexibility to flow with any pool shape, a frame of pavers not only adds pop but also provides a nonslip surface for the safety of swimmers. If soaking up the sun is a fair-weather favorite, pool-surrounding pavers can be extended to accommodate chaises and chairs. And if you are lucky enough to have a stream running through your landscape, paving a small bridge results in big charm.

ACCENTING ASCENSIONS A sloped lot usually requires additional planning, but it also provides the opportunity to add interest. Areas of ascending and descending landscape can reap the benefits of rough-hewn retaining walls and smooth-stone steps. Easing navigation through the landscape, stone steps are especially elegant along walkways winding through groomed gardens.

DRESSING UP DRIVEWAYS While most of the hardscape trends covered here focus primarily on back-of-home attractions, it's important to remember that first impressions are lasting. And what better way to welcome family and friends than leading them up a meticulously manicured path to your home? Whether a classic cobblestone or a contemporary cut-stone design, a professionally paved driveway creates immense curb appeal. In addition, because pavers' durability typically outperforms that of standard concrete, you can count on pulling up to paved perfection year after year.

Whether you are looking to simply create a cozy courtyard or more elaborately design your own private paradise, hardscapes help pave the way to realizing your outdoor design dreams.«

Ready for Relaxing

THIS SMALL FAMILY loves to entertain and cook for friends and relatives, so they needed to optimize the limited space in their backyard to accommodate a large number of guests. To prevent the space from feeling too open, designer Jason Horton broke the project into zones, including kitchen, fireplace, and pool (not shown) areas.

The kitchen area is fully functional, from the grill with warming drawer and storage to the beer tap, refrigerator, and ice maker. Countertops and seating walls throughout the yard provide plenty of space to congregate in every distinct section, so family and friends feel cozy and not crowded.

Learn more about this designer at
www.greenviewlandscape.com.«

DESIGNER
Jason Horton
Greenview Landscape
Design
9571 Charlotte Highway
Fort Mill, SC 29707
803.548.9730

SPECIAL FEATURES
Pool, fireplace

PRODUCTS USED
Flooring: Belgard
Hardscapes Cambridge
Cobble three-piece
Wall Stone: Glen-Gery
Landmark manufactured
stone veneers
Countertops: Tennessee
flagstone
Grill: Viking
Refrigerator: Viking
Ice Maker: Viking
Lighting: Vista

PHOTOGRAPHER: ZACK BENSON

All Fired Up

WHEN THIS COUPLE in Charlotte, North Carolina, decided to build an outdoor kitchen and living area, they called Bill Zemak of Overstream Landscape, Inc., who asked them a variety of questions regarding their cooking and entertaining habits and preferences. Then based on their answers, he designed a custom live-in zone featuring an open cooking floor plan that allows for lots of countertop space as well as working and serving room. The homeowners also wanted to include an exterior seating area, fireplace, swimming pool, and water feature as part of the overall design.

The backyard's 18-foot drop-off and the need to remain within a flood-plain line presented the biggest design demands. Zemak's solution was to build the outdoor living area and kitchen on top of a raised patio, giving a beautiful view of the natural area in the back of the yard.

One unique feature of the kitchen is the pavers, which are used for the flooring and the countertops. Zemak finished the space with everything needed for a great backyard barbecue: a grill, smoker, refrigerators, drop-in cooler, warming drawer, access doors, and sink. Ready to fire up the fun, the couple is thrilled with the end result. *Learn more about this designer at www.overstreaminc.com.*«

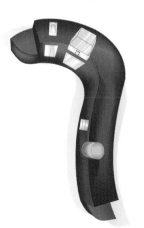

DESIGNER
Bill Zemak
Overstream Landscape, Inc.
Indian Trail, NC 28079
704.226.8836

SPECIAL FEATURES
Outdoor kitchen with grill, smoker, refrigerators, drop-in cooler, warming drawer, access doors, and sink

PRODUCTS USED
Flooring: Belgard Dublin Cobble pavers in Fossil Beige
Countertops: Belgard Dublin Cobble pavers in Fossil Beige
Refrigerators: BBQ Galore
Grill: BBQ Galore
Smoker: Big Green Egg
Warming Drawer: BBQ Galore
Storage Drawer: BBQ Galore
Drop-In Cooler: BBQ Galore
Access Doors: BBQ Galore
Paper Towel Holder: BBQ Galore

PHOTOGRAPHER: CHIPPER HATTER

Fun for the Family

With kids in high school and college, quality time matters to this tight-knit clan. They all love cooking and spending time outdoors, so they changed their underused backyard into a griller's paradise. The redesigned space is the place to be for family gatherings and entertaining the kids' friends.

Designer Jack Dorcey planned the kitchen to serve as the center for all outdoor activities. Having a limited side yard with which to work, the homeowners did not want a huge patio that spread too far from the house. Instead, a unique curved-edge patio creates enough space for a large double grill with a built-in bar that provides seating for five. Long gone are the days of the grill tucked into the corner, with the cook's back to the guests. Backyard cooking is all about the social experience of preparing the food, and with this design, everyone can be a part of the fun. The outdoor kitchen and fire pit are great for the family because they give the parents and kids an activity to do together outside.

The stainless-steel cabinetry maintains a sleek aesthetic and is able to withstand Minnesota's fluctuating weather extremes. An integrated ice chest keeps refreshments cool all day. Lighting built into the kitchen and throughout the surrounding landscaping ensures this intimate retreat is open all hours. *Learn more about this designer at www.landscapedesignstudios.com.*«

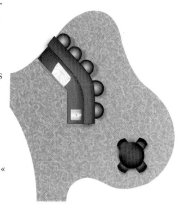

DESIGNER
Jack Dorcey
Landscape Design Studios
2482 Mayfair Ave.
White Bear Lake, MN 55110
651.239.7038

SPECIAL FEATURES
Grill with built-in bar seating, stainless steel cabinets with integrated appliances

PRODUCTS USED
Cabinetry: Medium Rare
Flooring: Belgard Dublin pavers
Countertops: Blue River Limestone
Lighting: Outdoor Lighting Concepts
Backsplash/Tile: Blue River Limestone
Grill: Medium Rare
Ice Chest: Medium Rare
Trash Drawer: Medium Rare

PHOTOGRAPHER: CHIPPER HATTER

A Natural Fit

The Klisters love to cook and entertain, so they wanted to build an impressive outdoor kitchen to match their passion. When they contacted designer Rob Schroth of Schroth Landscaping, LLC, their goal was to replace their old deck with separate patio areas that flowed together naturally and could be enjoyed by groups large and small.

Such an intricately layered patio is not built easily. To begin, Schroth had to reroute pipes and outlets on the outside of the house with precise care. He also replaced 3 feet of spongy subsoil with compacted stone to provide a stable, durable base for the pavers.

The kitchen area has a stainless-steel grill, side burner, sink, and cabinets, as well as outlets for additional appliances. It is 8 inches lower than the surrounding areas, so when the chef stands, he or she is level with guests who are seated in tall chairs. A sitting area complete with an umbrella, stools, and a foot rest offers a cozy place to unwind. Pavers set on a curve create a unique look. Another notable custom feature is the diamond pattern of the accent tiles on the walls throughout the different areas. The overall result is a kitchen area, fire-pit area, seat walls, planting areas, and sitting areas that coalesce gorgeously in the great outdoors.

Learn more about this designer at www.schrothlandscaping.com.«

DESIGNER
Rob Schroth
Schroth Landscaping, LLC
117 Pine St.
Brillion, WI 54110
920.756.9800

SPECIAL FEATURES
Patio pavers used in the walls for style consistency; stainless-steel appliances, sink, and storage; trimwork around the counter topped with a highlighting paver; electrical outlets cut into the wall block; an umbrella and stools for added comfort

PRODUCTS USED
Cabinetry: Bull
Flooring: Belgard Urbana
Countertops: Concrete
Grill/Side Burner: Bull
Lighting: Nightscape
Backsplash: Weston Wall
Wall Seats: Belgard
Walls: Belgard Weston Stone

All Decked Out

THIS SMALL FAMILY likes to entertain their much larger extended family on special occasions, but their confined exterior quarters were not too accommodating. So when it came time to design their outdoor kitchen, these fun-loving homeowners made sure to specify extra counter space for food preparation, seating for dining, an outdoor refrigerator, and cabinetry near the grill—all meshed into a functional, entertainment-friendly layout.

Landscape architect Gary Blanford determined that the best option to meet all of their needs was to build not one, but two spaces: the smaller zone contains the kitchen and hosts intimate gatherings; the larger zone (not shown) accommodates up to three dining tables for big parties. Dividing the space also allowed three large trees to be preserved.

Cleverly incorporated design features include earthy colors accented with ambient light emanating from hidden fixtures. Large planters next to the steps create a transition between the two patios. Natural stepping-stones lead across the lower portion of the yard to steps that lead up to the elevated patio. Hardscape elements such as the walls and steps mingle beautifully with softer plantings and warm illumination to create a perfectly cozy atmosphere that beckons guests season after season. *Learn more about this designer at www.blanforddesign.com.«*

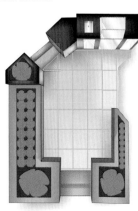

DESIGNER
Gary Blanford
Blanford Design,
Landscape Architects
and Contractors
575 W. Crossroads
Parkway
Bolingbrook, IL 60440
630.771.0775

SPECIAL FEATURES
Belgard BelAir Wall with stone face in ashlar pattern, granite-topped columns to match countertops, spacious transition steps between upper and lower patios, Turkish marble paver tiles aligned to unify upper and lower patios

PRODUCTS USED
Flooring: Turkish marble
Countertops: Double Granite
Grill: Cal Flame
Refrigerator: Cal Flame
Lighting: Integral, Kichler
Wall: Belgard BelAir
Other: Cal Flame pullout trash bin drawer, Cal Flame two-drawer deep storage, Sony outdoor speakers hidden within the plantings
Wall Seats: Belgard

PHOTOGRAPHER: CHIPPER HATTER

Open-Air Oasis

THIS FAMILY OF five likes to entertain regularly, but their backyard was inadequate for accommodating many guests. To make use of the lush surroundings, they removed the old deck and filled a low area of the yard that held water with limestone. They also hired designers Karen Timm and Nick Hubbard of Beary Landscaping, Inc., to create an all-new outdoor kitchen that makes innovative use of their space.

Choosing to keep the dense oaks in the backyard spared the trees but also restricted space. To offset the limited square footage, the custom kitchen-and-grill area features Belgard BelAir walls that double as seating by incorporating a backsplash bar with stools. All of the seating centers around a large natural-gas and wood-burning fireplace. A special rubber-mulch pathway leads safely from the kitchen area to a play zone for the children (not shown).

The trees also hindered the use of the outdoor kitchen for evening entertaining by blocking light and attracting bugs. Now, an automated insect mist system guards the perimeter of the yard with plant-based organic insecticides, maintaining a pest-free zone. Uplights in the living space, downlights in the trees, and path lights brighten up the space for use into the night. *Learn more about this designer at www.bearylandscaping.com.*«

DESIGNERS
Karen Timm and
Nick Hubbard
Beary Landscaping, Inc.
15001 W. 159th St.
Lockport, IL 60491
815.838.4100

SPECIAL FEATURES
Belgard walls and
pavers, Barbeques
Galore kitchen
components,
Mist Away Outdoor
Insect-Control System

PRODUCTS USED
Cabinetry: Built using
Belgard BelAir wall
Flooring: Belgard Arbel
pavers
Countertops: Autumn
brown granite with
suede finish
Grill: BBQ Galore 40-inch
natural-gas grill with
rotisserie and two
40-inch double access
doors
Fireplace: Belgard
Elements Collection
Other: Pull-out stainless-
steel garbage can and
built-in paper-towel
dispenser

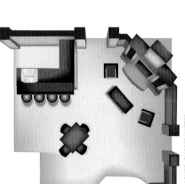

PHOTOGRAPHER: CHIPPER HATTER

Lakeside Living

SOUTH CAROLINA'S LONG summers and a lakeside lot provided the perfect plot for year-round entertaining for this family of five. So when they undertook a home expansion, they included an outdoor makeover as part of the renovation. The upstairs addition created a covering for the new *alfresco cucina*.

With the space allotted, the homeowners had several requests for designer Elizabeth Beyers of DCI Home Resource as she finished out the space. Their main desire was for lots of seating for optimal guest comfort. Beyers achieved this by incorporating bar seating for eight-plus people that allows easy conversation thanks to the U-shaped island bar top. Table seating for six under the covered area offers even more dining and lounging space. All seating was positioned to allow unobstructed traffic flow from the house, through the entertaining and pool area, and to the boat dock.

With the grill placed for proper ventilation, the entire cooking area took shape. The orientation of the island opening toward the cooking wall creates an easy transition from the cooking area to the serving and seating area at the bar. With all of the design details filled for the updated outdoor space, these homeowners are ready to continue their lakeside-living lifestyle. *Learn more about this designer at www.dcihomeresource. com.«*

DESIGNER
Elizabeth Beyers
DCI Home Resource
1300 South Blvd., Suite C
Charlotte, NC 28203
704.926.6000

SPECIAL FEATURES
Unusually large outdoor kitchen, separate cooking and serving areas, U-shaped island with seating for eight or more

FEATURED PRODUCTS
Cabinetry: Danver stainless steel
Flooring: Travertine tile
Countertops: Baltic Brown granite
Grill: Viking
Oven: Viking
Warming Drawer: Viking
Ice Maker: Viking
Backsplash: Baltic Brown slab granite

MEMBER OF
SEN DESIGN GROUP

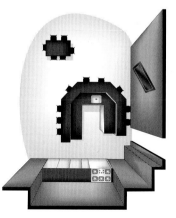

PHOTOGRAPHER: ELIZABETH BEYERS

West-Coast Cucina

Marilyn C. Gardunio, CKD, of J.B. Turner & Sons had formed a two-year relationship with these homeowners over the course of an extensive design and remodel of their Alamo, California, home. So when the family purchased a vacation home in Coronado, they again turned to her and the design team at J.B. Turner & Sons to transform the 1970s Tudor-style house into a comfortable coastal-style home.

Taking into consideration how the family would use the space as well as the surrounding waterscape, Gardunio planned out a full outdoor living area for them to fully enjoy the warm Southern California weather.

The space began as a narrow, bare concrete slab, but Gardunio got to work on creating a full kitchen and entertaining area. The kitchen area includes a sink, ice maker, refrigerator, barbecue, and lots of cabinet space. In the entertaining area, fulfilling the clients' desire for a focal point, Gardunio designed a dramatic waterfall fireplace that anchors a gathering spot for the family and their guests. She also positioned the feature so that the master bedroom has a view of it.

By transforming an area that was lacking into a luxurious outdoor living area, Gardunio has once again designed a space this family can enjoy with one another and friends. *Learn more about this designer at www.jbturnerkitchens.com.*«

DESIGNER
Marilyn C. Gardunio, CKD
J.B. Turner & Sons
1866 Pleasant Valley Ave.
Oakland, CA 94611
510.658.3441

SPECIAL FEATURES
Waterfall fireplace, abundant cabinetry

FEATURED PRODUCTS
Cabinetry: Atlantis Cabinetry
Flooring: Tile Shop porcelain tile
Countertops: Soapstone
Sinks: Blanco
Faucets: Delta
Grill: Viking
Refrigerator: Perlick
Fireplace Tile: Ann Sacks
Lighting: Ultra Lights

MEMBER OF
SEN DESIGN GROUP

PHOTOGRAPHER: CHIPPER HATTER

Florida Fresh

LIVING IN NAPLES, Florida, these homeowners wanted to increase and improve the time they spend enjoying the wonderful weather for which the area is famous, but they lacked finished outdoor living space. To create cooking quarters and a lounge area for accommodating family and friends, they hired designer Matt Chadwick of Chadwick Outdoor Kitchens.

Designing it as a true extension of the home, Chadwick configured the space so it could be completely enclosed when needed. Fully equipping the alfresco area with a host of appliances—even a dishwasher—and other amenities, such as a stone-wall-mounted flat-screen TV, further blurs the lines between indoors and out.

In the designated kitchen area, Chadwick installed a surplus of base cabinets—all made of marine-grade stainless steel. Manufactured by Danver, the cabinets' clear-coat finish protects them from everyday nuisances such as fingerprints and water spots as well as more-serious threats from harsh weather.

Finishing the new outdoor living area with such flourishes as a farmhouse sink and a Mediterranean-tile backsplash, Chadwick fulfilled these Floridians' dream of a fresh-air living space.
Learn more about this designer at www.chadwickoutdoorkitchens.com.«

DESIGNER
Matt Chadwick
Chadwick Outdoor Kitchens
6342 Lee Ann Lane
Naples, FL 34109

SPECIAL FEATURES
Farmhouse sink, dishwasher, marine-grade base cabinets

FEATURED PRODUCTS
Cabinetry: Danver stainless steel
Countertops: Granite
Sink: Farmhouse stainless steel
Grill: Fire Magic
Hood: Vent-A-Hood
Refrigerator: Marvel
Wallcovering: Stone
Backsplash/Tile: Kurtz Homes

PHOTOGRAPHER: MATT CHADWICK

Eco Canyon Retreat

DESIGNER KRISTINA URBANAS SPENCER of Setting the Stage Interior Design starts each project by considering the three basic "green design" elements: energy conservation, energy efficiency, and renewable energy. And this Pasadena 1958 midcentury ranch's green patio remodel was no different. Her task: completely gut the backyard and create an entertainment area with the canyon as the focal point and design inspiration—all while utilizing the American Society of Interior Designers and U.S. Green Building Council green guidelines for residential remodeling.

The family loves to entertain, so Spencer crafted 600 square feet of living, dining, and kitchen space without creating an excessive carbon footprint. The concrete patio contains 40 percent fly ash, and the drought-tolerant landscaping includes 1,500 square feet of synthetic lawn. Modular tanks on the property capture and store rainwater.

Spencer had Los Angeles graffiti artists makeover the lackluster masonry wall, creating a custom family-centric mural. Topping off the area, the patio cover's roof is made up of six solar panels that provide some of the electricity for the house. All of these design elements conserve in concert for a living space that is environmentally sound. *Learn more about this designer at www.settingthestageinteriordesign.com.*«

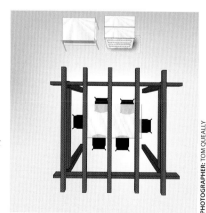

DESIGNER

Kristina Urbanas Spencer
Setting the Stage
Interior Design
1950 Canyon Close Road
Pasadena, CA 91107
626.590.8429

SPECIAL FEATURES

"Green" exterior living, dining, cooking space; seamless transition from patio to canyon vista; drought-tolerant landscaping and rainwater collectors; mix of metal cactus plant sculptures and real cacti in the landscape

PRODUCTS USED

Grill: Viking Range
Patio Cover: Created with solar panels
Graffiti Wall: Arco and Ruets
Patio: 40 Percent fly ash concrete
Synthetic Lawn: Jack Turf

PHOTOGRAPHER: TOM QUEALLY

History in the Making

A HISTORIC HOUSE donated to the Red Cross in the 1960s and serving as current headquarters for its regional chapter, the Craven estate is also used for weddings, events, and location filming. Transformed by the Pasadena Showcase House of Design in 2010, the property's outdoor kitchen and garden were designed by Jan Ledgard, CKD, CBD, of Yorkshire Kitchens Inc.

Two of Ledgard's biggest challenges were the restrictions that come with a historic property and implementing "green" design principles. To start, she cleared the area except for the liquid amber tree, which served as a beautiful natural canopy. She then installed terrace steps and a deck around the tree—both made of eco-friendly Timbertech.

The kitchen is outfitted with a grill and refrigerator, concrete countertops, weatherproof cabinetry, and a recycled-glass counter with the Red Cross symbol etched into it. Other glass features include agave-patterned tabletops, a gate, stepping-stone lights, and a water feature. Finishing touches included a retractable awning, eco-friendly landscaping and lighting systems, and a pergola.

All the design details worked in harmony to restore this historic property to peak condition for its multiple purposes. *Learn more about this designer at www.yorkshirekitchens.net.«*

DESIGNER
Jan Ledgard, CKD, CBD
Yorkshire Kitchens Inc.
849 A Foothill Blvd.
La Canada, CA 91011
626.345.1750

SPECIAL FEATURES
Weatherproof cabinetry, recycled-glass counter and tables, retractable awning

FEATURED PRODUCTS
Cabinetry: Atlantis Outdoor
Flooring: Timbertech
Handrail: Teak of Teak
Countertops: Concrete and glass
Sinks: Elkay Martini Glass stainless steel
Grill: Twin Eagles
Glass Features: Ultraglass
Lighting: Lighting Innovation low-energy lights
Refrigerator: Twin Eagles
Hardware: Atlas Homewares

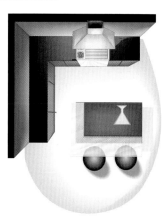

PHOTOGRAPHER: ANDREA BRICCO

California Dreamin'

WANTING A BACKYARD to reflect his family's lifestyle, this Los Angeles homeowner desired an outdoor design that would accommodate 2 or 200 guests, put technology at his fingertips, and allow him to use the space year-round. These requirements were simple compared with those of his 9-year-old daughter, who provided Firoozeh Khorrami of Design Schematic with her drawings and wish list, which included a water slide and a cabana that housed a TV, snack bar, and refrigerator for cool drinks.

By taking into consideration the existing landscape and canopy of the beautiful oak trees, Khorrami designed a pool, spa, cabana, and kitchen that not only exceeded their requests but also added character to the house. The pool—which features iridescent glass tiles, a water slide, and a Baja bench with an inlaid ceramic-tile monogram—provides a beautiful waterscape view from the cabana and kitchen. Family and friends can watch TV while enjoying a cool drink at the bar in the cabana or lounge beside the fire pit while the host heats up the grill in the fully equipped outdoor kitchen.

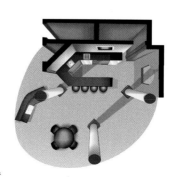

A dry riverbed, carefully selected lighting, state-of-the-art audio equipment, and Internet access on all the TVs are just a few of the details that made this outdoor design a California dream. *Learn more about this designer at www.designschematic.com.*«

DESIGNER
Firoozeh Khorrami
Design Schematic
P.O. Box 570072
Los Angeles, CA 91357
818.888.6179

SPECIAL FEATURES
Integrated indoor/
outdoor design, custom
lighting, stainless-steel
outdoor cabinets

PRODUCTS USED
Cabinetry: Stainless steel
Countertops: Granite
Grill: Viking Range grill
and cooktop
Refrigerator: Viking
Ice Maker: Viking
Backsplash/Tile: Walker
Zanger
Plumbing Supplies:
Fergusons
Furniture: Century
Furniture

PHOTOGRAPHER: MAGNUS STARK

English Countryside

BUILT IN 1927 by architect Paul Williams, this English manor four-acre estate had fallen into disrepair in recent years. The grounds had been neglected, with an old barn and stables sitting abandoned. Ready to revive the estate to its full elegance, the owner decided to repurpose the stable as a guest cottage and add an outdoor kitchen and terrace. He hired the perfect designer for the job: English-born Jan Ledgard, CKD, CBD, of Yorkshire Kitchens Inc.

A huge double-trunk pine is the centerpiece of the entire space, so Ledgard built a lava-rock planter around the tree (just visible to the right in the main photograph of the kitchen, right). He used a natural stone "bouquet canyon" for terrace floor. Both materials were found on the grounds. The kitchen features a Twin Eagles grill and a margarita mixing station as well as a bar station—all set by the luxe materials. The outdoor kitchen cabinetry features Accoya wood doors, and the Brown Rainforest marble countertops have been sandblasted to give them the look and texture of leather.

A plethora of furniture provides plenty of dining and lounging spots, and the indoor/outdoor room leading from the terrace into the cottage is outfitted with a host of entertainment amenities. *Learn more about this designer at www. yorkshirekitchens.net.*«

DESIGNER
Jan Ledgard, CKD, CBD
Yorkshire Kitchens Inc.
849 A Foothill Blvd.
La Canada, CA 91011
626.345.1750

SPECIAL FEATURES
Accoyo outdoor wood cabinetry, fire pit, custom mural

FEATURE PRODUCTS
Cabinetry: Four Seasons
Flooring: Natural Stone and concrete
Countertops: Rainforest Brown textured marble
Sinks: Elkay
Faucets: Elkay
Grill: Twin Eagles
Margarita Machine: Twin Eagles
Lighting: Lighting Innovation
Hardware: Atlas Homewares

PHOTOGRAPHER: ANDREA BRICCO

Patio Parties

THIS CHARLOTTE, NORTH CAROLINA, family wanted an outdoor living area that would indulge the man of the house's passion for grilling and allow them to enjoy the area together as well as with guests. Their requirements included covered cooking and dining areas, an additional seating area, and an outdoor fireplace. To pull it all together, they called on Tony Everett of Custom Land Design.

Due to the home's steeply sloped lot, the design challenge was to maximize the use of the backyard by retaining a grassy play area for the children while adding a 30 x 40-foot outdoor living space. So Everett designed different levels to break up the space; then he incorporated a fireplace into the back retaining wall, creating a stunning focal point (not visible in photos).

Everett layered complementary products, such as a combination of stone and Belgard's Dublin Cobble pavers, to achieve a natural aesthetic that is warm and inviting. He also built several planters to soften the hardscapes with greenery, and he installed an arbor and planting bed with shrubs adjacent to the dining area. Fast forward to today, and the family is delighting in their new alfresco space, which is made all the more enjoyable thanks to Dad's delicious backyard barbecues! *Learn more about this designer at www.customlanddesign.com.*«

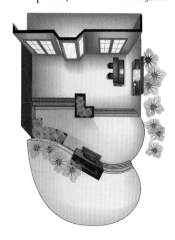

DESIGNER
Tony Everett
Custom Land Design
3210 Sunset Drive
Charlotte, NC 28209
704.333.5815

SPECIAL FEATURES
Outdoor kitchen with grill, smoker, ice maker, sink, and outdoor fireplace with woodbox

PRODUCTS USED
Flooring: Belgard Dublin Cobble pavers in Fossil Beige accented with Tennessee fieldstone and Tennessee flagstone
Countertops: Tennessee flagstone with snapped edge
Grill: Fire Magic grill with pot burner
Smoker: Big Green Egg
Ice Maker: U-Line
Wallcovering: Tennessee fieldstone and Tennessee flagstone

PHOTOGRAPHER: CHIPPER HATTER

Rain or Shine

DESIGNER
Matt Chadwick
Chadwick Outdoor
Kitchens
6342 Lee Ann Lane
Naples, FL 34109

SPECIAL FEATURES
Powder-coated wood-
grain finish over
stainless-steel cabinets,
built-in consideration of
hurricane codes

FEATURED PRODUCTS
Cabinetry: Danver
stainless steel with wood
powder-coat finish
Flooring: Pavers
Countertops: Granite
Grill: Lynx
Sideburner: Lynx
Refrigerator: Marvel
Warming Drawer: Lynx
Hood: Vent-A-Hood

WHEN THESE HOMEOWNERS decided to add on to their
Pelican Marsh home in Naples, Florida, they expanded their
plans to the outdoors as well. An outdoor kitchen was just
what they needed to make the most of their locale in the
Sunshine State. There was only one problem: despite all of
the beautiful weather that earned Florida its nickname, the
region is susceptible to seasonal hurricanes, which can wreak
havoc on standard-built structures. To ensure that their
new space remained standing season after season, year after
year, they called on designer Matt Chadwick of Chadwick
Outdoor Kitchens.

Chadwick designed the layout with Lynx, Marvel, and
Vent-A-Hood built-in appliances that meet hurricane codes.
High-end surfaces such as granite countertops add a touch
of indoor-level luxury. Also fulfilling the homeowners'
wishes, Chadwick was able to give the cabinets a wood-grain
appearance while providing marine-grade
weatherproofing. Using an incredibly
realistic powder-coated wood-grain finish
over stainless-steel cabinets, the space
gained the appeal of wood minus the
maintenance. And because the cabinets
come with a lifetime warranty, the owners
can enjoy their outdoor kitchen worry-free,
no matter what the weather! *Learn more
about this designer at
www.chadwickoutdoorkitchens.com.*«

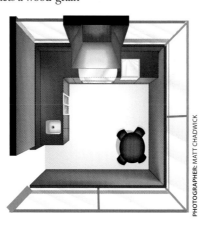

Stone Sanctuary

SURROUNDED BY A heavily wooded terrain, these Connecticut homeowners wanted an alfresco addition that would allow them to take in the serene scenery in a more comfortable setting. To carve out culinary and open-air living rooms on their lot, they sought the skills of renowned outdoor designer Michael Gotowala, president of Preferred Properties Landscaping & Masonry.

With their list of wants and needs complete, the homeowners had one more request of Gotowala: to have the project completed and guest-ready within six weeks' time for an upcoming wedding. Getting started, the Preferred Properties team laid stone and brick to define the space and then continued with these materials to create the kitchen, fireplace, and spa, which is positioned to take advantage of the fireplace. Polished yellow granite provides a stunning countertop.

Thoughtful details such as a wine and beverage nook as well as the finishing touches of lush landscaping and accent lighting helped Gotowala exceed these homeowners' expectations. And they were doubly thrilled that their new stone sanctuary was complete in time to serve as the setting for a beautiful September wedding. *Learn more about this designer at www.outdoorlivingct.com or www.outdoorkitchendesigner.com.«*

DESIGNER
Michael Gotowala
Preferred Properties
Landscaping & Masonry
1456 Highland Ave.
(Route 10)
Cheshire, CT 06410
203.250.1030

SPECIAL FEATURES
Natural materials and palette to complement the surrounding landscape, stone fireplace, spa built into a wall of fire, well-appointed kitchen with wine and beverage nook

FEATURED PRODUCTS
Cabinetry: Danver
Countertops: Polished yellow granite
Grill: DCS by Fisher & Paykel 48-inch grill
Refrigerator: Summit
Lighting: Preferred Properties Landscape & Masonry
Backsplash: Stone and granite
Pull-Out Trash: Danver
Spa: Sundance
Fire Jars: Planika

PHOTOGRAPHER: MICHAEL GOTOWALA

All-Weather Retreat

THIS ACTIVE SOUTHERN California family of five wanted to create a fun, functional outdoor kitchen that would maximize their stunning Coto de Caza hillside views. They envisioned the great room and loggia/patio functioning as a single, fluid space. To achieve their dreams, they called on RoomScapes, Inc.

To make way for a larger interior/exterior living area, the design team extended into the outdoors from the family room. They allocated zones for and designed the outdoor kitchen, bar, and wine room. A pass-through window to the interior allows access to the bar and wine spaces and enhances the flow from indoors to outdoors, as do matching counter and backsplash materials on the indoor bar and outdoor worktop. The design team also recommended interior-quality materials, effectively fusing the warm feeling of the Tuscan-styled living quarters into the outer realm.

Additional custom details include space heaters integrated into the new tongue-and-groove ceilings, lockable-roller stainless-steel enclosures to protect media equipment from the elements, and dramatic LED-backlit onyx stone serving counters. Custom niches, artwork, and iron details further solidify this interior-meets-exterior motif, which beautifully blurs the boundary between indoors and out. *Learn more about this designer at www.roomscapes.net.«*

DESIGNER
RoomScapes, Inc.
23811 Aliso Creek
Road, #139
Laguna Niguel, CA 92677
949.448.9627

SPECIAL FEATURES
Custom stainless-steel and cherry cabinetry, integrated media systems, LED-backlit onyx service counters

PRODUCTS USED
Cabinetry: Danver for exterior, Wood-Mode for interior
Flooring: Design MGM, Inc., travertine
Countertops: Design MGM, Inc., granite on lower; onyx on upper
Sink(s): Houzer
Faucet(s): Grohe Ladylux Pro
Refrigerator: Perlick
Grill: Lynx grill, Fire Magic side burner
Hood: Lynx
Lighting: Harbor Electric, Inc., LED lighting with onyx top
Warming Drawer: Lynx
Wallcovering: Design MGM, Inc., stacked stone; UBC wall texture
TV Enclosure: Häfele
General Contractor: United Builders of California

MEMBER OF
SEN DESIGN GROUP

PHOTOGRAPHER: CHIPPER HATTER

Open-Air Living

This Cheshire, Connecticut, family's home sits on a lovely lot, but the landscaping was lacking fun and functionality. Frequent entertainers and lovers of the outdoors, they hired designer Michael Gotowala, president of Preferred Properties Landscaping & Masonry, to transform their backyard terrain into an open-air oasis.

On the list for the layout: a kitchen, pool house, pool, sundeck, fireplace with pizza oven, and plenty of seating. To blur the lines between house and addition, Gotowala built the structure out of matching stucco and stone. To add architectural interest, he designed the add-on with an arched roof. By extending the roofline outward and incorporating repeating arched entry points, he exceeded expectations while also framing great vistas into the backyard. Also adding visual interest, great detail was given to the night-lighting design by lighting expert Gotowala.

With the kitchen covered yet open, it can accommodate large gatherings in any weather. And with an infrared Solaire grill, warming drawer, power burner, two Summit refrigerators, stainless-steel cabinetry, farmer's sink and faucet, and nearby pizza oven, the owners can do so much more than just flip burgers. No longer just a mirage, this outdoor oasis is everything the homeowners desired and more. *Learn more about this designer at www.outdoorlivingct.com or www.outdoorkitchendesigner.com.*«

DESIGNER
Michael Gotowala
Preferred Properties
Landscaping & Masonry
1456 Highland Ave.
(Route 10)
Cheshire, CT 06410
203.250.1030

SPECIAL FEATURES
Arched stucco rooftop, fully equipped kitchen, fireplace with pizza oven

FEATURED PRODUCTS
Cabinetry: Danver stainless steel
Pavers: Uni-Lock Brussels
Countertops: Polished yellow granite
Grill: Solaire Infrared Grills
Power Burner: Alfresco Grills
Warming Drawer: Alfresco Grills
Oven: Alfresco Grills
Refrigerators: Summit
Pizza Oven: Tuscany style
Lighting: Preferred Properties
Wallcovering: Stucco
Backsplash: Stucco

PHOTOGRAPHER: MICHAEL GOTOWALA

Raised Expectations

NESTLED ON A wooded property in the Northeast, this outdoor living space started with a simple request to remove a deck's side rail to accommodate a grill, burner, and sink. But as these Greenwich, Connecticut, homeowners continued working with designer Michael Gotowala, president of Preferred Properties Landscaping & Masonry, their expectations began to rise—figuratively and literally.

Desiring a more complete cooking area as well as immediately accessible dining and lounging zones, the homeowners quickly expanded the project's scope to also include a wraparound kitchen island with bar seating and a beverage center, a designated dining area, and a focal-point masonry fireplace with a Tuscany-inspired pizza oven—all of which are located 30 feet in the air on this second-level deck.

Building such an elaborate setup on the second level was no simple task but well worth the effort. By doing so, the owners gained a greater level of seclusion, privacy, and security. The natural materials and neutral tones blend beautifully with the landscape, which is heavily wooded and includes a pond on the property. Below the deck, an outdoor wine-tasting "room" is a great starting place for guests before moving upstairs to settle in and enjoy the scenery. *Learn more about this designer at www.outdoorlivingct.com or www.outdoorkitchendesigner.com.*«

DESIGNER
Michael Gotowala
Preferred Properties
Landscaping & Masonry
1456 Highland Ave.
(Route 10)
Cheshire, CT 06410
203.250.1030

SPECIAL FEATURES
Second-level locale, stone wraparound island, masonry fireplace with Tuscany-style pizza oven

FEATURED PRODUCTS
Cabinetry: Danver stainless steel
Flooring: Opaq decking
Countertops: Polished granite
Sink: Famer's sink
Faucet: Moen
Grill: DCS by Fisher & Paykel 48-inch infrared grill
Side Burner: Sol-Aire
Refrigerator: Summit
Lighting: Preferred Properties Landscaping & Masonry
Wallcovering: Stone

PHOTOGRAPHER: MICHAEL GOTOWALA

Relaxing Retreat

WANTING A BACKYARD getaway complete with an outdoor kitchen and living area, these Palmyra, Pennsylvania, homeowners called on Eric Allebach of the Greenskeeper to create a setup where they could retreat and relax.

To take advantage of the sloped lot as well as to create a sense of separation from the house, Allebach added a paved walkway that runs across the backyard to steps that lead down to the kitchen and living areas. The pergola-covered kitchen serves as the centerpiece, with a sitting area and fireplace along one side. Stone benches resembling Celtic walls offer additional seating and act as retaining walls.

Parallel counters made of stacked stone define the cooking area. The homeowner-built wooden pergola overhead is accented with string lights that enhance the festive atmosphere. Top-of-the-line outdoor appliances—including a stainless-steel rotisserie grill on one side and a sink, drop-in refrigerator, storage cabinets, and prep space on the other side—make outdoor meals easier than ever.

With the project complete and complementary of their home and swimming pool, these homeowners are able to enjoy their outdoor kitchen day and night in almost any season. *Learn more about this designer at www.lawnsbyeric.com.*«

DESIGNER
Eric Allebach
The Greenskeeper
162 Bell Road
Palmyra, PA 17078
717.838.5299

SPECIAL FEATURES
"Celtic wall" benches, outdoor fireplace, pergola-covered outdoor kitchen

PRODUCTS USED
Countertops: Painted poured concrete
Paving: Belgard Dublin Cobble pavers in Fossil Beige
Counter and Bench Seating: "Celtic wall" in Oxford Charcoal
Fireplace: Fire Rock
Fireplace Enclosure: Fieldstone

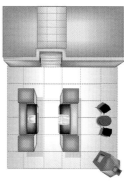

PHOTOGRAPHER: CHIPPER HATTER

Outdoor Entertaining

THESE HOMEOWNERS WANTED an entertainment-worthy outdoor environment. As parents of two teenagers, they also needed a place to keep their children occupied. To satisfy their desires for an outdoor entertaining utopia, the homeowners called on Bill Zemak of Overstream Landscaping & Irrigation.

Though the homeowners knew they wanted an outdoor living space complete with kitchen, pool, and patio, they didn't have specific design requirements. This meant the task of fashioning a space from scratch to suit their needs fell to Overstream. To realize the homeowners' dreams, the designers began by incorporating a system of drain lines throughout the yard. These lines lead to a water reclamation system, where water is recycled to irrigate the landscape. The team then excavated the pool and built the outdoor kitchen. A cozy sunken sitting area with a fireplace is ideal for entertaining.

A large wood pergola provides shade, and a swim-up bar invites swimmers to indulge in refreshments without having to leave the cool waters. The completed project, finished in a mere 13 weeks, is an enticing space that lures all to luxuriate in the great outdoors. *Learn more about this designer at www.overstreaminc.com.*«

DESIGNER
Bill Zemak
Overstream Landscaping
& Irrigation, Inc.
P.O. Box 1215
Matthews, NC 28106
704.226.8836

SPECIAL FEATURES
Outdoor kitchen built over water reclamation system, swim-up bar

PRODUCTS USED
Flooring: Mega-Bergerac pavers, Low Country by Belard, Mega-Bergerac large square pavers for coping
Walls/Fireplace: Celtik Wall by Belgard, stone veneer
Countertops: Dublin Cobble pavers by Belgard
Cooktop/Range: Barbeques Galore
Refrigerator: Avanti
Lighting: Copper brick lights, copper post lights for pergola
Drop-In Cooler: Barbeques Galore

PHOTOGRAPHER: CHIPPER HATTER

Patio Perfection

Aʟʀᴇᴀᴅʏ ᴘʟᴇᴀsᴇᴅ ᴡɪᴛʜ their extraordinary poolscape and pretty vistas, these Connecticut homeowners initially decided to simply tackle a patio-paver repair. But as they surveyed their backyard setting, they realized there was one way they still wanted to improve their open-air living area.

With the pool providing plenty of fun and the multi-tiered terrace to lounge on while taking in the landscape, it was only dinnertime that became a downer because it required them to head indoors. So they hired designer Michael Gotowala, president of Preferred Properties Landscaping & Masonry, to build in an outdoor grill setup to complement the existing hardscape and extend the leisure experience.

The bent L-shaped outdoor stone island Gotowala installed adds interest to the lower level by filling the previously empty spot between twin staircases. The island's two-level countertop offers significant surface space surrounding the grill for mealtime prep work and serving of the finished fare. A stainless-steel rack system built into the stone is perfect for barbecuing ribs.

By implementing their exemplary masonry techniques and niche for knowing just what their clients want, Gotowala and his Preferred Properties masons perfected this already incredible outdoor area. *Learn more about this designer at www.outdoorlivingct.com or www. outdoorkitchendesigner.com.*«

DESIGNER
Michael Gotowala
Preferred Properties
Landscaping & Masonry
1456 Highland Ave.
(Route 10)
Cheshire, CT 06410
203.250.1030

SPECIAL FEATURES
Stainless-steel grilling racks, bent L-shaped island

FEATURED PRODUCTS
Grill: Viking
Open Racks: Stainless steel
Stone Work: Preferred Properties Landscaping & Masonry

PHOTOGRAPHER: MICHAEL GOTOWALA

Sea-Level Living

PRIME PROPERTY FOR good reason, beach homes beckon you outside by appealing to the senses. The lulling sounds of rolling waves, the beauty of a seemingly eternal body of water, the salty smell of evening breezes, and the tickle of changing terrain underfoot all make waterfront setups particularly peaceful. So with sand and sea bumping up to their backyard, these Connecticut homeowners were ready to max out their space for outdoor living. To take on the transformation, they hired designer Michael Gotowala, president of Preferred Properties Landscaping & Masonry.

Multiple terraces of stone and granite patios feature a breakfast nook, seating under a sail-inspired cloth shade, fire pit, and hot tub installed in stone. The outdoor kitchen's design is especially distinct for two reasons: one, it is built-in and fully finished with stone and granite, and two, the space is sunken into the landscape to block the wind and protect it from the elements.

Outfitted with all the appliances needed for gourmet grilling in the great outdoors, additional amenities such as the gas fireplace for warmth and ambiance as well as a granite surround for seating complete this open-air kitchen for optimal outdoor living. *Learn more about this designer at www.outdoorlivingct.com or www.outdoorkitchendesigner.com.*«

DESIGNER
Michael Gotowala
Preferred Properties
Landscaping & Masonry
1456 Highland Ave.
(Route 10)
Cheshire, CT 06410
203.250.1030

SPECIAL FEATURES
Sunken stone design, granite surrounds, gas fireplace

FEATURED PRODUCTS
Cabinetry: Danver stainless steel
Flooring: Stone and granite
Countertops: Polished granite
Sink: Low-profile lobster sink with pullout hose underneath
Grill: Capital 40-inch grill
Warming Drawer: DCS by Fisher & Paykel
Refrigerator: DCS by Fisher & Paykel
Beverage Center: Summit
Fireplace: Stone fireplace with Lenox gas insert

Alfresco Entertaining

TARZANA, CALIFORNIA, LIES within the San Fernando Valley just outside of Los Angeles. It boasts a storied history, including the fact that it was once home to Edgar Rice Burroughs, author of the Tarzan stories, which served as the inspiration behind the town's name. The city also enjoys nearly year-round temperate weather, which means that there are options aplenty for outdoor entertaining in this location. And this Tarzana home is no exception.

As the second home to a business owner, this dwelling serves as an escape from the harried stress of day-to-day demands. Designed by David Cordon of Absolute Custom Landscape and outfitted by Fire Magic, purveyors of high-end grills and outdoor entertaining appliances, this outdoor kitchen is any entertainer's dream. A refrigerator, deluxe grill, side burner, blender, and bar caddy allow for the preparation of any culinary delight, ranging from the simple poolside burger to the complexities of a feast fit for a gourmand. The facade of the prep and cooking area is clad in stucco to complement the home, and accent lighting illuminates the space when dusk steals the daylight. Stone provided by Masonry Club surrounds the alfresco kitchen and invites guests to lounge in flip-flops or to simply kick off their shoes and stroll barefoot.
Learn more about this contributing designer at www.rhpeterson.com.«

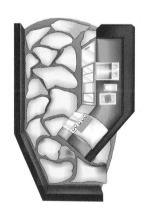

DESIGNER
David Cordon
Absolute Custom
Landscape
2500 Huntington Lane
Redondo Beach, CA
90278
310.379.4754

CONTRIBUTING DESIGNER
Robert H. Peterson

SPECIAL FEATURES
Block-style kitchen complete with glass-tile surround, accent lighting, outdoor entertaining experience with blender and bar caddy

PRODUCTS USED
Grill: Fire Magic
Side Burner: Fire Magic
Refrigerator: Fire Magic
Blender: KitchenAid
Stone: Masonry Club

PHOTOGRAPHER: ANDY MOORE

Culinary Couture

IN LAS VEGAS, where residents enjoy an average of 320 days of sunshine a year, cooking and dining alfresco is a way of life. Paragon Pools custom designed this outdoor kitchen to transform a traditional portable barbecue area into a welcoming sitting space. Desiring an outdoor cooking and dining area to accommodate large gatherings, this homeowner wanted the convenience of entertaining his guests while preparing his culinary delights. The L-shaped kitchen, with its large bar area, invites guests to visit with the backyard chef while he prepares the feast.

The counter is equipped with accent and directional lighting and multiple electrical outlets for appliances. Built-in remote controls for the pool, spa, and fountains are located within easy reach. A decorative retractable umbrella provides shade. To keep the activities going well into the evening, a gas fireplace adds ambiance, as well as a place to toast marshmallows.

The countertop and fireplace are accented with the same earth-tone Tuscany tiles as the pool, spa, and fountain, and the exterior stucco finish matches the house. *Learn more about this design team at www.paragonpools.net.*«

PARAGON POOLS
Joe Vassallo Jr.
2461 Professional Court,
Suite 110
Las Vegas, NV 89128
702.251.0500

SPECIAL FEATURES
Dual-burner grill with rotisserie; dual-burner side griddle; ice chest cooler; refrigerator; gas fireplace; accent and directional lighting; retractable umbrella

CATAGORY
Custom

PRODUCTS USED
Capitol Grill units; GE Profile refrigerator

The Great Outdoors

This Louisiana family leads an active lifestyle, frequently entertaining poolside and hosting dinner parties and game-watching get-togethers. Because many of their social events spill into the outdoors, they wanted to prime the area for alfresco entertaining.

For the transformation, they hired Kevin Harris, FAIA, of Kevin Harris Architect, LLC. By renovating a garage, Harris carved out connected but clearly delineated spaces for a cabana, cook's nook, and bathroom. Adjacent to the swimming pool, the outdoor kitchen serves both as a year-round grilling area and as a shaded spot that offers intimacy while still providing clear visibility of the kids in the pool. An oversize opening adjoining the sitting area and the kitchen lets conversation flow among the cook and guests, and seating with tables in both spaces further aids the intermingling.

Earthy, complementary finishes of green granite countertops, sage-painted cabinetry, stainless-steel appliances, and brick flooring combine for a comfortable yet indoor-outdoor ambiance. A series of matching sage shutters opposite the appliance wall opens up to allow views to the yard and pool beyond.

Upping the convenience factor even more, the attached bathroom features a granite-tiled shower and hand-painted ceramic sink—just two of the many design details that welcome this family and their guests into the great outdoors.

Learn more about this designer at www.kevinharrisarchitect.com.«

DESIGNER
Kevin Harris, FAIA
Kevin Harris Architect, LLC
451 E. Airport, Suite A
Baton Rouge, LA 70806-4832
225.924.7450

SPECIAL FEATURES
Shuttered wall that opens for views of the yard and pool; high-end finishes; suite of appliances; attached bathroom

PRODUCTS USED
Cabinetry: Custom cabinets painted sage green
Flooring: Brick
Countertops: Green granite
Sink: Custom stainless-steel sinks
Faucet: Kohler
Cooktop: Gas grill cooktop
Refrigerator: GE
Backsplash: Green granite
Other: Movable shutters

PHOTOGRAPHER: CHIPPER HATTER

An Outdoor Experience

For this North Carolina family, their outside living space ranked low on their list of style standards. Desiring all the accoutrements for alfresco entertaining at its finest, they hired Brian M. Kuchinski of Peaceful Ponds to complete an outdoor overhaul.

Achieving proper drainage presented the greatest out-of-doors challenge. Essentially working inside a box—an older yard framed with brick walls and plagued by flooding—Peaceful Ponds had to regrade the land, install drains, and control the pitch of the hardscape perfectly. The laser level and transit helped, but ultimately, it was the precision in installation that made it all work in the end.

The design's multiple levels flow beautifully, with sitting walls and steps providing visual continuity and function. The focal point is a custom river-rock fireplace with sitting wall, which is a gathering spot for friends. Other notable features include a unique fountain, which incorporates a reclaimed wine barrel from Napa Valley, and a double-grill station featuring a stainless-steel Bull grill and a Weber Big Green Egg—a grill master's dream combination.

In the end, Peaceful Ponds provided an outdoor kitchen that incorporates fire, water, landscaping, hardscaping, lighting, and drainage—every element of the outdoor experience this family imagined. *Learn more about this designer at www.peacefulponds.net.*«

DESIGNER
Brian M. Kuchinski
Peaceful Ponds
9000 Arbor Glen Lane
Charlotte, NC 28210
704.643.6456

SPECIAL FEATURES
Custom river-rock fireplace with sitting wall, one-of-a-kind fountain made using a reclaimed wine barrel from Napa Valley, double-grill station

PRODUCTS USED
Cabinetry: Bull stainless-steel doors
Flooring: Belgard Hardscapes' Mega Arbel Smokey Mountain with Mega Bergerac Fossil Beige border
Countertops: Tennessee flagstone in tan and brown from Blue Max Materials
Grill: Bull Angus stainless-steel grill with rotisserie, Weber Big Green Egg
Lighting: Custom low-voltage lighting throughout outdoor area
Backsplash: Tennessee flagstone in tan and brown from Blue Max Materials

PHOTOGRAPHER: MICHAEL VALENTINE

Outdoor Kitchen Oasis

FOR THIS FAMILY of five, frequent entertaining is a way of life—and not just with friends. Business associates are also often on the guest list, so these homeowners were ready to step up the presentation from simple patio to outdoor kitchen oasis. To make the transformation, they hired Darin Brockelbank and his design team at Metro GreenScape, Inc.

Utilizing the existing patio, Brockelbank focused on extending the space in ways that would allow for function and fun, plenty of seating, and easy traffic flow. Here's how he did it: a central semicircular raised bar accommodates up to six seated guests at a time. The grill was placed at the far left to prevent overheating the seating area. The refrigerator and drop-in ice chest were placed on the opposite side to keep cold beverages close at hand. The sink was placed in between the grill and refrigerator for equal accessibility to chef and guests, and abundant counter space provides a proper service area. Located next to the kitchen, an open space connecting the countertop to the fireplace houses a place for trash cans, recycling, and firewood.

With all the amenities one could need in a summer kitchen—plus a few extras—this family and their guests love the newly appointed patio. *Learn more about this design team at www.metrogreenscape.com.«*

DESIGNER
Metro GreenScape, Inc.
5019 Wilkinson Blvd.
Charlotte, NC 28208
704.504.0980

SPECIAL FEATURES
Drop-in ice chest; half-circle raised bar area to accommodate up to six people; designated area for storage

PRODUCTS USED
Cabinetry: BBQ Galore stainless-steel access doors
Flooring: Belgard Hardscapes' Dublin Cobble pavers in terra-cotta and Fossil Beige
Countertops: 2-inch Tennessee natural flagstone from Blue Max Materials
Sink: 18-inch stainless-steel from Lowe's
Faucet: Moen stainless-steel
Grill: Grill Master
Refrigerator: Summit
Lighting: Alliance low voltage
Other: Drop-in ice chest

PHOTOGRAPHER: CLEAR SKY IMAGES

Cabos "Comfort-scape"

THIS GLOBE-TROTTING LAS VEGAS family yearned to capture their favorite resort destination, Los Cabos, Mexico, at home. Paragon Pools was able to re-create the essence of the place by incorporating the vibrant outdoor style with the mixture of modern and Old World Mexican architecture, tiles, fabrics, color, accent pieces, and plantings. The theme is carried throughout the entire yard and pool area. At Paragon Pools, this is called a "Comfort-scape," where designers re-create a special place, providing a sense of solace through views from in the home, landscaping, and pool design.

Vivacious colors of red, blue, orange, green, and yellow are splashed across the Comfort-scape—on walls, pillows, tiles, pottery, and cushions. The raised entertainment area overlooks the numerous water features that pour into the pool, providing delightful and soothing sounds, as well as visual appeal. An authentically tiled wood-burning pizza oven is the centerpiece of the outdoor Mexican-inspired culinary space. The family spends endless evenings preparing homemade pizzas for their friends or relaxing on the large built-in terra-cotta-tiled bench accented with throw pillows. *Learn more about this design team at www.paragonpools.com.*«

PARAGON POOLS
Joe Vassallo, CBP
2461 Professional Court
Ste. 110
Las Vegas, NV 89144
702.251.0500

SPECIAL FEATURES
Built-in cooking and preparation area; built-in seating bench; outdoor dining table and chairs; oversize retractable umbrella; terra-cotta tile

CATAGORY
Backyard

PRODUCTS USED
Built-in wood-burning pizza oven; four-burner gas grill with side burner; outdoor refrigerator

Only the Best

WITH TWO CHILDREN in tow, these North Carolina homeowners spend much of their leisure time outdoors. Often, they do it in the company of close family and friends. To design a space that reflects their tastes for the finer things and fulfills their entertainment needs, they hired Darin Brockelbank and his design team at Metro GreenScape, Inc.

The main construction challenge Brockelbank faced: minimal access into and out of the backyard. His solution: strategically timed deliveries of materials that prevented filling up the street or the homeowners' driveway. Because the space also limited the kind of equipment he could use, the project took slightly longer than normal—14 instead of the usual 8 days.

Despite the challenges presented in logistics, the homeowners and designer ensured the project's success with a thoughtful floor plan and by not skimping on high-quality materials and products. The homeowners chose top-of-the-line DCS appliances by Fisher & Paykel and specifically requested the added feature of a rotisserie with their grill. Underfoot, Belgard Hardscapes' Dublin Cobble pavers look stunning while standing up to outdoor wear and tear.

Because the family's outdoor kitchen was created with only the best, the end result is even better than they imagined. *Learn more about this design team at www.metrogreenscape.com.«*

DESIGNER
Metro GreenScape, Inc.
5019 Wilkinson Blvd.
Charlotte, NC 28208
704.504.0980

SPECIAL FEATURES
Top-of-the-line outdoor appliances, including a grill with a rotisserie

PRODUCTS USED
Flooring: Belgard Hardscapes' Dublin Cobble pavers
Grill: DCS by Fisher & Paykel
Refrigerator: DCS by Fisher & Paykel

PHOTOGRAPHER: CLEAR SKY IMAGES

Celebration Central

THIS FUN-LOVING TEXAS couple loves nothing more than opening their home to their large extended family. Their married children also love to entertain and stage parties here on a regular basis. So when the time came to remodel their Dallas residence, the homeowners made certain to slot in an exterior kitchen and living area that would effortlessly extend the fun to the great outdoors.

The challenge for designers Ana Seyffert and Carlos Gallego of Spun Creative Group was to devise a layout with a fluid transition from indoors to out. The outside living room, the owners emphasized, needed to be as comfortable as their interior quarters. Also, the sleek contemporary design required unobtrusive support posts for the 16-foot cantilevered awning, granting a clear view of all areas. To achieve this, the designers used cables strung from the top of the metal frame and imbedded them in a thick concrete wall in three places. A rectangular opening softens the profile, while a concrete flowerbed housing bamboo plants borders the back of the wall.

A linear burner in a stainless-steel fire-pit table lights up the night. The table combines form and function—when it's not in use, the installation serves as a coffee table. To avoid heat transfer onto the rest of the metal table, the burner is flanked by two rectangular pieces of white marble. Now the parties are always hopping at this remade home! *Learn more about these designers at www.spungroup.com.*«

DESIGNERS
Ana Seyffert and Carlos Gallego
Spun Creative Group LLC
6607 Desco Drive
Dallas, TX 75225
972.392.7176

SPECIAL FEATURES
Semicircular concrete wall with a 16-foot cantilever awning; kitchen includes an adjacent living space with stainless-steel fire pit

PRODUCTS USED
Cabinetry: Kollyn Hakol
Flooring: Concrete tile
Countertops: Silestone
Sink: Julien
Faucet: IKEA
Cooktop Cart: DCS
Grill: KitchenAid
Refrigerator: Summit
Lighting: Casa Vieja
Other: Sparks Modern Fires linear burner system

Dream Design

WITH PLENTY OF their leisure time spent in the open air, this family of four desired a setup suited to their recreational style. Two priorities for the project: adding a screened-in porch and designing the husband's dream kitchen. To fulfill their wishes, they hired designer D. Scott Reister, RLA, ASLA, of TG&R Landscape Group.

The challenge for the porch was integrating it into the existing architecture. So Reister created a small transitional screened-in space that flows into a larger open-air terrace. Using brick that matches the house visually unites the old and new living areas.

The outdoor kitchen was designed around a centrally located fire pit (not shown). Guests can watch and interact with the chef, making the space an ideal spot for entertaining.

Other unique elements in this design are the eco-friendly measures that were taken. For example, the paver selection allows rain to permeate and flow into plants rather than being wasted as runoff. With their dream kitchen complete, this family is spending even more time together in the great outdoors. *Learn more about this designer at www.tgrlandscape.com.*«

DESIGNER
D. Scott Reister, RLA, ASLA
TG&R Landscape Group
745 Kinghurst Drive
Rock Hill, SC 29730
803.325.1010

SPECIAL FEATURES
Screened-in porch, radial design; large terrace; eco-friendly pavers

PRODUCTS USED
Flooring: Belgard Environmental
Countertops: Bluestone with chiseled edge
Grill: Kalamazoo
Refrigerator: Kalamazoo
Lighting: Vista

MEMBER OF
SEN DESIGN GROUP

Southwest Grandeur

NESTLED WITHIN ARIZONA'S desert canyons is an outdoor kitchen that reflects the majesty of its setting and makes its homeowners feel like kings of their domain. Seemingly contradictory is the fact that this impressive space manages to be grand but inviting, cutting-edge yet classic. How did the designer accomplish such a feat? By pairing high-end outdoor appliances with elegant materials and a cozy corner fireplace.

When first drawing up designs for this stone sanctuary, the homeowners wanted something that would provide the perfect recreation spot for their large family but not be jarring against the vibrant red-and-orange hues of their surroundings. To infuse warmth into the space, they chose rich red stones for the structure of the patio and tan polished concrete for the floor. While wall lanterns illuminate the work spaces, it is the corner fireplace—with a built-in stone and marble bench—that casts a glow over the patio. A table for four hosts family dinners under the stars.

The cooking takes place on two FireMagic stainless-steel grills, with dual side burners nestled between them. Meal preparation is done on marble countertops. There is a FireMagic minifridge, ensuring that everything the homeowners need is at their fingertips. With the fireplace separating these areas, the visual result is a sprawling work space in a corner of the yard. «

SPECIAL FEATURES
Majestic backdrop of Arizona desert; two FireMagic stainless-steel grills; dual side burners; minifridge; marble countertops; polished concrete flooring; stone structure

PRODUCTS USED
Flooring: Polished concrete
Countertops: Marble
Grill: FireMagic stainless-steel grills with dual side burners
Refrigerator: FireMagic minifridge
Lighting: Wall lanterns and corner fireplace

Pigment and Pattern

AS AN OWNER of Mission West Kitchen and Bath—a distributor of fine architectural hardware, plumbing fixtures, decorative lighting, and custom cabinetry—and Mission Tile West—a tile provider renowned for its unique selection of fine handcrafted ceramics, terra-cottas, and stones—Thano Adamson knew a thing or two about achieving one-of-a-kind kitchen styles using tile. After applying that knowledge to help countless clients, he decided to bring his work home with him.

When designing his own backyard entertainment area, his goal was to create a space intimate enough for hosting close friends and family that was also brimming with personality. To achieve this atmosphere, he arranged the floor plan with the kitchen along one wall, outfitting it with amenities such as an oil-rubbed bronze sink, a grill, and a pizza oven. Next, he turned his primary focus to pigment and pattern. It was this combination of color and textures that sets the scene and steals the spotlight in this outdoor design. Rusty orange honeycomb floor tiles radiate warmth. They also tie into the decorative tiles trimming the tile backsplash along the kitchen wall.

Adamson's use of pigment and pattern dressed up his patio exactly as planned. *Learn more about this designer at www.missionwest.biz and www.missiontilewest.com.*«

DESIGNER
Mission West Kitchen and Bath
Thano Adamson
905 Mission St.
South Pasadena, CA 91030
626.799.3503

SPECIAL FEATURES
Dominant theme of pigment and pattern achieved with abundant use of brightly hued tiles in rusty orange and green; pizza oven

PRODUCTS USED
Cabinetry: Green wood doors with brick accents
Flooring: Honeycomb-patterned tile
Countertops: Green granite
Sink(s): Oil-rubbed bronze prep sink
Grill: Gas turbo grill
Other: Pizza oven

Verandas and Vistas

WHETHER IN A newly built beach house on the coast or settled on the east-side state line, residents of sunny Southern California enjoy enviable weather just about year-round. As a result, the most prime real estate includes properties that take outdoor living up a notch, making it less of an option and more of a way of life. It was that very concept that drew these homeowners to move to the Golden State and, more specifically, to purchase this particular property.

With the outdoor kitchen designed as part of a large, open-air veranda, the homeowners could foresee a future full of entertaining with views of the green vista beyond. And thanks to the luxurious materials, suite of appliances, and thoroughly modern design, they could do so without sacrificing style or function.

Large, elongated slabs of white granite and oversize white tile flooring keep the atmosphere bright, and the back wall's wide expanse of mirrors reflects natural light throughout the covered patio. Glossy slate-colored and ash-wood cabinetry add an upscale, contemporary flair, while the stone island base and accent column tie into the outdoors. Seating on the other side of the island allows guests to gather around while the cooks are at work and provides the perfect spot to relax and enjoy the meal.«

SPECIAL FEATURES
High-end, luxury materials; modern aesthetic; suite of full-size appliances

PRODUCTS USED
Cabinetry: Custom
Flooring: Oversize tile
Countertops: Granite
Sink: Oversize trough sink
Cooktop: Jenn-Air four-burner induction
Oven: Jenn-Air
Refrigerator: Jenn-Air

California Modern

INCORPORATING AN OUTDOOR living space is certainly commonplace in California, but opening up a substantial portion of the structure to the great outdoors was an absolute must for these homeowners when they decided to build their West Coast dream home.

Long drawn to the beach, the couple chose this place because of its ocean views and year-round favorable climate. And to make the most of it, they designed their home with plenty of open-air spaces for their own enjoyment and for entertaining their frequent houseguests. Two distinct spaces—both overlooking an L-shape minimalist reflection pool—allow for cooking and dining in one area and lounging and sipping cocktails in the other.

With high-end finishes such as a stone wall, top-of-the-line appliances, one-of-a-kind pendant lights, and a dining table for eight, the kitchen portion is the perfect place to host dinner parties. And with the operable wall system, it can be fully opened to the outdoors or closed off in cooler weather. Adjacent to the summer kitchen, an even-larger lounge area features a substantial bar with bar stools, space to mingle, and a massive custom-built L-shape couch for the ultimate in relaxation. No longer just California dreamin', this couple made their ultimate open-air home a reality.«

SPECIAL FEATURES
Operable wall system to open or close off the kitchen; alfresco lounge area; reflection pool in minimalist style

PRODUCTS USED
Cabinetry: Custom
Countertops: Granite
Sink(s): Under-mount stainless steel
Lighting: Custom pendant lights

Natural Treasure

CHARACTERIZED BY ITS gorgeous Great Lakes and eye-appealing landscape, the state of Michigan is a sports enthusiast's paradise. Its crisp waters dotted by sailboats on summer days, Michigan is a primed-for-play location for outdoor recreation. For this reason, it's not surprising that outdoor kitchens are trending so heavily in this nature-loving locale. So when these homeowners decided to set sail with an outdoor kitchen, they wanted it to include as many features as possible to play up their inspiring pristine Michigan location.

Their wish list encompassed a host of show-stopping elements to help them entertain with elegance while enjoying the camaraderie of family and friends. Sports aficionados (especially when their favorite local teams are involved), they requested a comfy spot for prepping fun noshes and partying away on game day. But they also desired a dressed-up setting that would be equally fitting for more-formal get-togethers. After drafting an A-list designer to turn their dreams into reality, the owners sat back and watched their vision take shape.

Sporting a lineup of weather-ready appliances by KitchenAid, their new culinary zone is equal measures low-key and high-style. A standout design that blends beautifully with its setting, this game-changing culinary zone hits it right out of the park!

SPECIAL FEATURES
Stone pavers and island; KitchenAid appliances

PRODUCTS USED
Flooring: Stone pavers
Grill: KitchenAid
Side Burner: KitchenAid
Trash Bin: KitchenAid
Refrigerator: KitchenAid
Access Drawers: KitchenAid
Utility Drawers: KitchenAid

PHOTOGRAPHER: KITCHENAID

Pacific Getaway

WHEN THESE HOMEOWNERS were zeroing in on a West Coast vacation home, it was clear to them that being a hop-skip-and-jump away from the cool ocean waves sealed the deal. However, their dream wasn't complete until they built a poolside kitchen to take full advantage of the location's magnificent vista.

In this classic California setting, cherry cabinets are paired with stainless-steel KitchenAid appliances and an earthy tile on the countertops. The tile's rough-textured finish suits the surf and beachy atmosphere perfectly, making the homeowners feel like a part of nature rather than simply observers.

Ever the entertainers, the homeowners have found that their roomy kitchen island is the perfect place to rest a tropical drink or prepare a fresh-caught seafood dinner. It has plenty of room for friends to gather, too.

The open-air pergola overhead matches the natural beauty and finish of the wooden deck and permits a view of the evening stars. Its location, a step up from the pool area, ensures that the kitchen is its own defined space.

Not to get too wistful, however, this kitchen is still decked out with every modern convenience—a stainless-steel sink, fridge, cabinets, and grill (all by KitchenAid), and a roomy prep surface. It is this mix of the practical meeting the extravagant that the homeowners were going for when they envisioned their outdoor addition.«

SPECIAL FEATURES
State-of-the-art built-in appliances, use of natural textures and colors, large tiled island and countertops, cherry cabinets, wood deck and pergola, pool and beach view

PRODUCTS USED
Cabinetry: Cherry
Flooring: Exposed wooden deck
Countertop: Earthy rough-textured tile
Sink: Stainless steel
Faucet: Stainless steel
Grill: KitchenAid stainless steel
Refrigerator: KitchenAid stainless steel

New England Escape

WITH GREEN SURROUNDINGS and cool summers at their disposal, New England homeowners can enjoy the summer months without being driven indoors by sweltering heat. In fact, it doesn't take much more than the first blades of green grass after a harsh winter for New Englanders to begin enjoying the outdoors again.

When designing their new patio space, these Connecticut homeowners knew they wanted to create a grilling area that would blend with the natural setting outdoors. Having glimpsed too many eyesores cluttering their neighbors' properties—think big, bulky, black grills standing on gray concrete—they chose products and materials that had a more organic feel.

While the KitchenAid products make outdoor cooking a breeze, the brickwork and polished granite in earthy hues take center stage and offset the sometimes cold look that stainless steel can have. Built-in disposal and storage space means the homeowners don't have to worry about presentation when they are hosting their friends for a summer BBQ.

With a state-of-the-art grill complete with burners at their disposal, these first-time homeowners can try out a variety of recipes—whether they call for rotisserie or smoking or braising the meat. The feature of their outdoor patio they like most is the spaciousness of the workstation, which allows them to cook side by side.«

SPECIAL FEATURES
High-end outdoor kitchen products, including KitchenAid grill and burners; stone and brick features in natural hues that complement the outdoor space

PRODUCTS USED
Flooring: Brick
Countertop: Polished granite
Grill: KitchenAid stainless steel with double side burners

PHOTOGRAPHER: KITCHENAID

Suburban Sprawl

LUSH FOLIAGE SURROUNDS this attractive porch and patio, part of a home tucked into a quaint Virginia suburb. These homeowners knew that because of its poolside view, this was the perfect backyard to become the neighborhood hangout for their teenage kids and their friends.

Looking to outfit the space with all the necessities, the homeowners chose this stainless-steel suite of appliances by KitchenAid. Grill, fridge, and built-in refreshment center sit side by side, creating the ultimate plan for easy outdoor entertaining. The compact refreshment center is complete with sink, faucet, cutting board, and water filter. There's space for grilling tools and ingredients, too. The grill sports its own bells and whistles. Top of the line, this 48-inch model features an even-heat system—even the worst cook will find it almost impossible to burn dinner.

The porch, patio, and pool naturally split the outdoor living area into three separate zones for entertaining. The porch, built by the homeowners themselves, has classic lines and lets the beauty of the wood stand out naturally. With the porch's sitting area located so close to the cooking area directly below on the patio, conversation flows easily between these two zones.

By creating a space the whole family can enjoy, these East Coast homeowners have solidified themselves as the coolest parents on the block.«

SPECIAL FEATURES
Poolside deck and patio space, stainless-steel KitchenAid appliances and storage space, lush garden surrounding

PRODUCTS USED
Flooring: Brushed concrete;
Sink: KitchenAid stainless-steel sink
Faucet: KitchenAid stainless-steel outdoor faucet
Grill: KitchenAid stainless-steel 48-inch grill
Refrigerator: KitchenAid stainless-steel minifridge
Storage: KitchenAid stainless-steel built-in refreshment center

PHOTOGRAPHER: KITCHENAID

Deck Design

As any design pro will tell you, it's not how much space you have, it's what you do with it. By making the most of your outdoor living areas you can create the wow factor that impresses guests, no matter its size. When these New Jersey homeowners first began remodeling their home, they thought a small backyard would prevent them from extending their plans to the outdoor space. Their deck addition proved to be the perfect solution.

Equal parts function and fun, the deck is divided into several zones: a recreation spot, complete with a hot tub; a dining area; and a cooking area, which is decked out with state-of-the art grilling features. The natural wood creates a unified aesthetic that carries across the entire deck, with partitions that provide privacy from nearby neighbors. With easy accessibility to the house, the homeowners are able to prolong grilling foods into the cooler fall months.

The stainless-steel KitchenAid grill is the centerpiece. With three U-shape burners, a sear burner, two rotisserie burners, and a smoker box, it can handle the grilling chops of Bobby Flay himself; yet it is easy to use for this all-American family. A minifridge and refreshment center eliminate any running back and forth indoors, making outdoor cooking and dining a truly relaxing experience.«

SPECIAL FEATURES
Intimate family dining atmosphere created by portioned deck space; stainless-steel upgrades on grill, sink, and refreshment center

PRODUCTS USED
Flooring: Natural wood deck
Sink: KitchenAid stainless-steel sink
Faucet: KitchenAid stainless-steel faucet
Grill: KitchenAid stainless-steel 48-inch gril
Refrigerator: KitchenAid minifridge

Let the Good Times Roll

BUTTER YELLOW AND charming, this Covington, Louisiana, house is the pride of its owner. And while the homeowner has always set out a welcome mat at her New Orleans-inspired residence, she felt that something was missing—one special element that would round out the setting and make it complete. After consulting with a designer, she realized what was lacking was an outdoor kitchen. The backyard easily lent itself to the project, and with plans to also add a pool, the homeowner and the designer put their heads together to create an entertaining outdoor space.

First things first, the designer had to meet the homeowner's aesthetic requirements: a clean-lined layout with minimal geometry and plenty of open-air spaces for people to move about easily from one area to the other. Aside from the relatively pared-down look, the designer also had to integrate three separate—but equally important—elements: a cabana, a grill, and a bar. The cabana space includes a Belgard Elements grill island, which the owner routinely fires up during her famous patio parties. And speaking of the patio, the Belgard Mega-Lafitt beauty includes a Belgard Elements Bristol L-shaped bar outfitted with a sink, ice maker, beverage cooler, and plenty of storage space.

Now when the homeowner is ready to get the party started, it truly is as easy as 1-2-3!«

SPECIAL FEATURES
Cabana, grill built into bar, Belgard pavers

PRODUCTS USED
Cabinetry: Belgard
Flooring: Belgard
Countertops: Belgard

PHOTOGRAPHER: BELGARD

Miami Vice

WITH A TRUE weakness for all things alfresco, it was only a matter of time before this couple made the move to Miami. A few years ago, *Forbes* magazine ranked Miami "America's Cleanest City" thanks to the city's amazing air quality, vast green spaces, clean streets, and citywide recycling programs—a list of benefits that helped lure the couple. Of course, the endless entertainment hot spots for which Miami is also known didn't hurt either. But with coastal views of the Atlantic from their new prime property, they also wanted to entertain at home.

Frequent hosts of extended family and friends, the homeowners wanted to outfit their backyard with a complete kitchen featuring all of the amenities of the one indoors. Wanting only the best, they stocked their space with top-of-the-line Viking appliances.

Available in both freestanding and built-in options, the all-season setup they chose includes a grill with rotisserie burners, a side burner with a wok ring, and an additional side burner. Storage cabinets, a warming drawer, a refrigerator, and a freestanding beverage dispenser round out the meal-making mix. Plus, the heavy-duty casters on the unit let the good times roll.

If their passion for open-air entertaining was a dream before, it is now a full-time lifestyle for these new Miamians. *Learn more about these products at www.vikingrange.com.«*

SPECIAL FEATURES
Freestanding outdoor kitchen units with top-of-the-line Viking appliances

PRODUCTS USED
Cabinetry: Viking
Flooring: Tile
Grill: Viking grill with rotisserie burners
Cooktop: Two side burners, one sized for a wok
Warming Drawer: Viking
Refrigerator: Viking
Beverage Dispenser: Viking

Simple Entertainment

WHEN THESE HOMEOWNERS first moved into this Rochester, New York, ranch-style house, they were delighted to discover a backyard fireplace. However, after living there for a year and never using the fireplace once, they decided to add on a complete outdoor kitchen to make the space more inviting and conducive to entertaining. The first thing they did was extend the brick wall around the fireplace to accommodate stained-wood cabinets and slate-gray granite countertops. The countertops also have flecks of green, which echo the yard's trees and other plantings. Generous counter space that includes a peninsula makes prep work easy; guests can pull up stools to talk to the cook. The cabinets provide ample storage, so the homeowners don't have to run inside for supplies.

Designed to fit within pre-existing columns, the new outdoor kitchen space perfectly suits the style of the house, and leaves enough green space for the homeowners to garden and the children to play.

Outfitted with a stainless-steel dual sink, dishwasher, fridge, and oven, this outdoor kitchen has all the amenities of the one indoors without the drawback of being stuck inside a hot, stuffy, room on a beautiful day. With its easy access to the yard and the children's play area, it's no wonder that the space has quickly become the family's entertainment center.«

SPECIAL FEATURES
Red brick, stainless-steel oven, dual sink, fridge, and dishwasher; wood cabinets; slate-gray countertops; wood beams and rafters

PRODUCTS USED
Cabinetry: Wood
Countertops: Slate-gray
Sink(s): Stainless-steel, dual sink
Faucet(s): Stainless steel
Oven: Stainless steel
Refrigerator: Stainless-steel minifridge
Dishwasher: Stainless steel
Lighting: Wall lanterns and rafter lights

Modern Milieu

CONNOISSEURS OF BOTH modern art and the relaxed California lifestyle, this quintessential West Coast couple designed their dream house with several goals in mind. First and foremost, they gravitated toward a gallery-style floor plan with an open layout to display their vast collection of paintings and other art pieces. Next, they wanted to stay true to a sustainable philosophy to help protect the environment that they so much enjoyed. And lastly, they desired a design with all the amenities and extras to create an entertainment spot for the frequent guests they welcome into their home.

Once the house was complete, the couple was ready to apply those same principals to the exterior spaces. So they hired Mark Scott Associates to mirror the indoor's special style into the outdoor-living areas. A patio overlooking the expansive vista beyond features a built-in grill and cooking zone as well as dining and lounge seating, rounding out this home's artistic modern milieu.

The organically shaped pool reflects the blue sky above. The stone hardscaping that surrounds the pool and drought-resistant landscaping reduce water consumption. The pool and its stone surround also provide a perfectly pristine backdrop to display the showpiece of the design: the two-story art installation that pops color into the otherwise neutral palette. *Learn more about this designer at www.markscottassociates.com.*«

DESIGNER
Mark Scott Associates
2022 Orchard Drive
Newport Beach, CA 92660
949.852.1727

SPECIAL FEATURES
Built-in grill setup with dining and lounge seating, two-story modern art installation, organically shaped pool, fully stocked bar with glass-block bar wall, staircase for access to the home's second floor, drought-friendly landscaping and hardscaping

A Toast to Style

TAKING OUTDOOR LIVING above and beyond resort-level luxury, the alfresco atmosphere is the pièce de résistance on this stunning, sprawling estate.

Designed with meticulous attention to detail, Mark Scott Associates washed the landscape with specially chosen stone surfaces, a mix of polished and rustic woods, soft materials for seating, textural materials for aesthetic interest, and all the accessories that would adorn each zone's indoor counterpart. While all the accoutrements lend a warm, cozy feel, the lack of walls lifts the visual weight to retain the open-air, casual comfort.

All designed with views of the enviable poolscape—which is surrounded by lush landscaping, highlighted with accent lighting and made unique with a waterfall-spray hot tub—the various vignettes combine to create a complete entertainment package. The living area's focal point is the fireplace flanked by dual built-in custom armoires. High-end furniture made especially for the outdoors allows the owners and their guests to sit back and relax fireside. Just outside this space is the dining area, outfitted with both a formal dining setup for six as well as casual bistro tables for two. A toast to style, the bar features a flat-screen TV built into a custom cabinet with storage, a suite of top-of-the-line stainless-steel appliances, and everything needed for enjoying a drink with friends. The design's showpiece style is unlike any other. *Learn more about this designer at www.markscottassociates.com.«*

DESIGNER

Mark Scott Associates
2022 Orchard Drive
Newport Beach, CA 92660
949.852.1727

SPECIAL FEATURES

Open-air living area with fireplace flanked by dual built-in custom armoires; high-end furniture and accessories, such as formal and casual dining sets; bar-area flat-screen TV built into custom cabinet; suite of top-of-the-line stainless-steel appliances; luxe materials and finishes; lush poolscape with custom lighting and water features

SoCal Dreamscape

IF YOU THINK of the outdoors and adjectives such as sleek, high-tech, and palatial don't come to mind, then it's time to redefine how you see the it. That's exactly what these Southern California homeowners did when they hired Mark Scott and Associates to design an outdoor space that shakes up most people's conceptions of a backyard patio. Complete with an outdoor fireplace, bar, stone fountain, and amazing view, it would be easy to forget that this is only one portion of the home.

On festive occasions, the homeowners can now enjoy the game or serve drinks and a meal at their own custom bar. The tile bar, which features polished-marble countertops, seats seven. When that's not enough, extra seating is available at the adjacent dining table, which overlooks California's rolling hills. In order to serve the number of guests their patio can accommodate, the homeowners installed a state-of-the art stainless-steel grill and other outdoor kitchen amenities, such as a stainless-steel sink.

The fireplace, with its natural-color cut granite stone is warm and inviting, especially for holding conversations over wine on cool evenings. A pergola shades the area from the strong afternoon sunlight. Adding to the serenity that the home's view affords is a stone fountain that the homeowners enjoy as they listen to the sound of moving water. *Learn more about this designer at www.markscottassociates.com.«*

DESIGNER
Mark Scott Associates
2022 Orchard Drive
Newport Beach, CA
92660
949.852.1727

SPECIAL FEATURES
Fireplace with granite stones, stone fountain, bar with LED TV, polished-marble countertops, stone-tile floors, Doric columns

Creature Comforts

AFTER ADDING a wine cellar, these homeowners thought it would be wonderful to have an outdoor space in which to enjoy their favorite vintage with their family and friends. In addition to a multipurpose veranda suitable for large-scale entertaining, one of the clients, a fine artist, envisioned an open-air aesthetic melding a variety of motifs: rustic, tropical, transitional, and Victorian. In other words, the end result should be a grand celebration of eclectic decor.

To bring this project from vision to completion, they hired Neal's Design Remodel. Because the homeowners' association prohibited freestanding outdoor structures, the designer incorporated a decorative trellis into the plan that connects the house to the outdoor living area. The L-shape and C-shape contours of the established landscaping provided inspiration for the angular and circular design elements of the veranda. Primary to the space are a fully equipped outdoor kitchen and an oversize bar with plenty of seating. Outfitted with several fans for warm weather and a fireplace for the cool months, it lets the homeowners enjoy the space no matter the season.

Other interesting design elements include stone surfaces, a flat-screen TV, and a free-form bar sink that can be filled with ice and beverages when entertaining. With so many desirable amenities and creature comforts, these homeowners now have a great entertainment spot. *Learn more about this designer at www.neals.com.* «

DESIGNER

Neal's Design Remodel
7770 East Kemper Road
Cincinnati, OH 45249
513.489.7700

SPECIAL FEATURES
Fully equipped kitchen, stone fireplace, oversize bar with seating, flat-screen TV

PRODUCTS USED
Cabinetry: Cal Spa
Countertop: Glass Tile OE Casa California/ Tahoe noniridescent for countertop
Flooring: Emil Porforities Verde Grandino ceramic brick tile
Countertops: Granite, tile
Sink: Elkay Mystic stainless steel
Faucet: Moen Vestige
Grill: Cal Spa
Refrigerator: Cal Spa
Hood: Vent-A-Hood
Fireplace: Heat N'Glo Montana
Fireplace Façade: Tenneesse Mountain Ledge cultured stone

Successfully Restyled

WITH AN ACTIVE entertainment schedule and two boys in high school, this Austin family needed a backyard makeover to provide a welcoming yet practical space to enjoy time with both family and friends. With this in mind, they contracted with John Martin of Straight and Level Construction to help them create the backyard of their dreams. Working together, the owners and Martin designed an outdoor kitchen and stunning entertainment space—all within the tightly confined plot.

The main challenges came with reworking the existing terrain and incorporating a sink into the kitchen area. The solutions: altering the landscape with fill and concrete, and then tapping the water supply and drain mechanism from a garage sink. The cabinetry was framed out of lumber and supplemented with premanufactured drawer and storage units. This proved cost effective, including reducing labor costs, allowing them to direct more resources to other luxury elements, such as Venecia Fiorito granite countertops, dramatic travertine tile flooring, custom cedar corbels, a single-bowl oversize sink, two cable TVs and speakers tied to the house sound system, and a copper water sculpture emerging from the outer kitchen wall into the fountain. A 38-inch grill, separate infrared-burner grill, and Big Green Egg smoker cover all of the cooking needs.

If a project's outcome is measured by how frequently it is used and enjoyed, then this backyard's restyle is a sure success! *Learn more about this designer at www.straightlevel.biz.* «

DESIGNER

John Martin
Straight and Level
Construction
5905 Haydens Cove
Austin, TX 78730
512.577.9297

SPECIAL FEATURES

Venecia Fiorito granite countertops, two cable TVs and speakers connected to the home's sound system, a copper water sculpture emerging from the outer kitchen wall into the fountain

PRODUCTS USED

Cabinetry: Lumber frame with stock drawers and storage units
Flooring: Travertine tile
Countertops: Venecia Fiorito granite
Sink: Single-bowel oversize sink
Grill: 38-inch gas grill and separate infrared-burner grill
Smoker: Big Green Egg
Lighting: 10 downlights, Casablanca remote-controlled ceiling fan

PHOTOGRAPHER: FRANK KUHLMEIER

365-Day Design

THESE OHIO HOMEOWNERS relish hanging out in their backyard during the lazy days of summer. When they set about laying out their outdoor kitchen, however, they were dead-set on creating a space that would be just as cozy in the cold months as it was in the warm weather. The solution: an enclosed porch. But it had to appear as if it were an original part of the existing structure and not a mismatched addition. What's more, the walls had to be erected so as not to impair the view to the lake beyond.

Undaunted, Neal's Design Remodel team utilized new windows and screens designed to echo the home's proportions. The existing deck served as the footprint for the new porch, eco-consciously allowing the majority of the mature landscaping to remain intact. With the outdoor kitchen now positioned inside the new porch, the upgraded grill required a vented hood. To maintain symmetry, the venting pipe was routed around the center beam of the new roof. Additionally, a heat shield was installed between the chimney and the roof. The open-deck arrangement affords the unobstructed sightlines that the homeowners desired. On the wall opposite the chimney, a long bar-height counter was installed directly against the wall for a front-row seat to the view outside. Year-round entertaining—here it comes! *Learn more about this designer at www.neals.com.* «

DESIGNER
Neal's Design Remodel
7770 East Kemper Road
Cincinnati, OH 45249
513.489.7700

SPECIAL FEATURES
Screened-in porch for year-round living, edge-style bar top with seating for four overlooking backyard, built-in appliance suite with plenty of surrounding countertop prep space, full-wall stone backsplash

PRODUCTS USED
Countertops: Granite
Grill: Viking
Refrigerator Drawers: Viking

PHOTOGRAPHER: FRANK KUHLMEIER

Treasure-State Style

HOME TO YELLOWSTONE National Park and Glacier National Park, Montana has six tourism regions and endless possibilities for exploring the great outdoors. It is also home to some of the most avid outdoorsmen. Regardless of the season, residents of the Treasure State spend a lot of time in the great outdoors—hiking, biking, and fly fishing in the warmer months and skiing, snowmobiling, and dog sledding in the winter months.

For those nature lovers lucky enough to live in the state, the spectacular scenery is an everyday benefit—but not one to be taken for granted. In fact, this family of six desired an outdoor spot to relax even after working in the open air all day. Third-generation ranchers on their family ranch nestled in a mountainous region of Montana, they had a breathtaking view outside their door but were lacking a comfortable outdoor environment in which to unwind after a long day.

Choosing a modular prefabricated design from Harmony Outdoor Living, they were able to pick each element of their outdoor kitchen piece by piece. A grill was a necessity, of course, but the wood-fired pizza oven was a bonus and focal point of the design. A built-in wine rack, a raised countertop with seating, and the use of stone for a natural look round out this Treasure State-style outdoor kitchen. *Learn more about this company at www.harmonyoutdoorliving.com.* «

SPECIAL FEATURES
Stone-surround wood-fired pizza oven, built-in wine rack

PRODUCTS USED
Modular Outdoor Kitchen: Harmony Outdoor Living, Inc.
Flooring: Stone pavers
Countertops: Stone
Grill: ProFire
Pizza Oven: Harmony Outdoor Living, Inc.

Outdoor Oasis

DESIGNER
John Ripley
17825 SE 82nd Drive
Gladstone, OR 97027
503.593.0121

SPECIAL FEATURES
Raised bar with 54-inch round seating area, infrared heaters, surround sound, outdoor plasma TV, custom fire pit

PRODUCTS USED
Cabinetry: Island custom frame by Outdoor Kitchens
Countertops: Brown Antique granite with antiquing process by 3CM Granite
Sink: Eclipse Tiburon stainless-steel under-mount
Faucet: Eclipse Poseidon Gooseneck
Grill: Fire Magic Echelon with Magic Window
Fire Pit: Custom by FireGear

THIS OREGON FAMILY'S busy lifestyle led to their desire for an outdoor living space where they could relax and entertain in their own private oasis. Working with designer John Ripley of Outdoor Kitchens, they created a space unique to their lifestyle, location, and needs.

This custom outdoor kitchen includes all the features to please even the most accomplished gourmet. Features such as under-counter refrigeration, storage and trash compartments, a built-in ice chest, a sink, and the all-important grill with a sear zone and a rotisserie complete this fully functional kitchen. A full-length raised countertop gives guests a front-row seat to witness newly honed outdoor barbecuing skills. A unique feature of the beautiful granite countertop is its antiqued finish, which has a more natural look. The base of the island features a natural-stone veneer. The same finish appears on the sitting walls surrounding the pool area and the custom fire pit with a stainless-steel star burner.

This outdoor space can be enjoyed year-round by utilizing the covered area, the infrared heaters to keep warm and comfy even on chilly days, and the outdoor ceiling fan to enjoy a gentle breeze on those warm days. There is even an outdoor plasma TV connected to surround sound. Finally, there is the million-dollar view of majestic Mount Hood with the Clackamas River meandering through the valley below. *Learn more about this designer at www.outdoorkitchens.com.«*

Backyard Makeover

THERE ARE TIMES when an outdoor kitchen is the main focus of an outdoor project. But sometimes the design expands into so much more. One thing can lead to another, and that was definitely the case here.

While her husband was serving his country in Afghanistan, this homeowner was on a mission of her own: to have the backyard makeover completed by the time he returned home. So Outdoor Kitchens designer John Ripley joined the ranks to help create an open-air retreat where this special couple could relax together once reunited.

Putting a lot of thought into each feature, Ripley kept the options coming. Then husband, wife, and designer discussed them on a video-chat service over the Internet. Once all of the decisions were made and implemented, the end result was a big hit. All new hardscaping, decking, sitting and landscape walls, a wood-burning fireplace, and the L-shape kitchen blended together beautifully. The kitchen was placed in the center of the open area with a raised countertop, offering a great view of the fireplace and the surrounding property.

Now back home to his made-over backyard, this husband has a place for gathering with his wife, family, and friends for an evening fire and great food. It's good to be home! *Learn more about this designer at www.outdoorkitchens.com.«*

DESIGNER
John Ripley
17825 SE 82nd Drive
Gladstone, OR 97027
503.593.0121

SPECIAL FEATURES
New eating area on the deck, wood-burning fireplace, covered hot tub

PRODUCTS USED
Cabinetry: Island custom frame by Outdoor Kitchens
Countertops: Tropical Brown granite from 3CM Granite
Grill: AOG by R.H. Peterson
Refrigerator: Fire Magic
Veneer: Sawn Aslar stone

Vibrant California Paradise

THE ENDLESS SUMMERS for which Newport Beach is known make it the perfect spot for lavish outdoor living. The homeowners of this California home enjoy stepping off Newport's white-sand beaches into their own backyard resort. The home's sprawling crystal-blue pool and stone cabana are the perfect setting for them to entertain with lavish parties that can last well into the night.

The outdoor kitchen is fully equipped with a stainless-steel grill and grill hood, side burner, microwave, LCD TV, and minifridge. However, the unique touches added by the design team—Mark Scott Associates—elevates it beyond function. Lush, tropical plantings pop againt a backdrop of light-colored stone walls, granite countertops, and rustic wood cabinets. The swim-up pool bar with underwater stone stools makes guests feel as if they are at a luxury hotel. The bar also has the added benefit of uniting the pool and kitchen area so that the homeowners can chat with their guests while firing up steaks on the grill.

When not enjoying the pool or kitchen areas, the homeowners can kick back in the side sitting area, which has windows looking into the home's interior. But here they really enjoy the soothing view created by their opulent outdoor haven. *Learn more about this designer at www.markscottassociates.com.*«

DESIGNER
Mark Scott Associates
2022 Orchard Drive
Newport Beach, CA 92660
949.852.1727

SPECIAL FEATURES
Pool with swim-up bar, stone counters, granite countertops, rustic wood cabinets, stainless-steel outdoor kitchen appliances, LCD TV, exterior lighting

Layered-on Luxury

WITH THE YOUNGEST of their children finally off to college, this couple's attention no longer needed to focus solely on their kids. After more than 20 years of putting their children's wants and needs first, these empty nesters decided to redirect those resources to satisfying some of their own dreams and desires. They wanted to create a place where they could regroup and relax after a long day, reconnect with each other, and provide recreation for their friends—and, of course, their children when they came to visit.

Always appreciative of California's climate, there was no question that they would make this space for living outdoors. To transform their plain patio into a five-star summer kitchen, they hired Mark Scott Associates, which is known for its masterful designs—and this project was no exception. With an abundant use of natural stone and the thoughtful addition of wood panels on the ceiling, the area has a rustic yet high-end appearance that works well in the outdoor environment. Topped with handsome granite, the L-shape island offers a bar area and plenty of surface space for food prep and serving.

The revamped outdoor room is also outfitted for fun with a grill, a beverage refrigerator that can hold more than 100 cans and bottles, and a flat-screen TV that was custom-designed to flip down from the ceiling when in use and to retract back up when it's not needed. It's this layered-on luxury that the homeowners love so much. *Learn more about this designer at www.markscottassociates.com.*«

DESIGNER
Mark Scott Associates
2022 Orchard Drive
Newport Beach, CA
92660
949.852.1727

SPECIAL FEATURES
Abundant use of natural stone, beverage refrigerator that can hold hundreds of canned and bottled drinks, flat-screen TV that flips down from the wood-paneled ceiling

Wine-Country Haven

DEEP IN THE heart of Sonoma County sits this California dream house that's reminiscent of an Italian villa. With an enchanting view of the hills beyond, the lucky homeowners have transformed their outdoor patio in complementary fashion to its surroundings. The Alfresco suite of outdoor cooking appliances transforms this otherworldly space into one of function as well as beauty.

A 42-inch Alfresco AGBQ grill is built into the wood cabinetry. Countertops are marble. A stainless-steel side burner matches the finish of the grill and expands the cooking space. When not in use for preparing food for the grill, the center island becomes an intimate eating area. Accompanied by candlelight, the homeowners enjoy everything from quick lunches to dinner dates here. The party moves to a large dining table a few feet away when company comes.

The homeowners cite the distinct zones of the patio as one of its best features. In addition to the cooking and dining areas, the patio has a spot for lounging that is ideal when the homeowners want to curl up with a good book. Its focal point is the classic Venetian-styled pergola, which provides shade from the sunny-California rays. A cast-iron fireplace adds warmth and romance and makes the transition from day to night easy.

The flowering plants add their sweet scent to the air and make it hard for the homeowners to ever leave the magical place they have created «

SPECIAL FEATURES
Cast-iron fireplace, wooden counters and island, marble countertops, Alfresco grill and cook line, pergola and lounge area

PRODUCTS USED
Cabinetry: Wooden
Flooring: Concrete with stone accents
Countertops: Marble
Grill: Alfresco, 42-in. AGBQ stainless-steel grill
Lighting: Iron lantern and mounted iron-pillar lights

PHOTOGRAPHER: GORDON SWANSON

Serene Simplicity

AFTER DECADES OF living the high life and enduring the stress of fast-paced careers in the hustle and bustle of Los Angeles, this California couple decided to reinvent their lives after retirement. While they had always loved spending time outdoors, the opportunity used to come in small spurts during the occasional long weekend away. Ready to get away permanently, they left the city behind them and headed north. Their retirement plan: to live a more simple, quiet life of relaxation.

It didn't take long before they found the perfect lot—a secluded, sloped spot in a lush setting right along the Pacific. Working with an architect known for his award-winning modern designs, the couple helped direct the clean-lined, light-filled, contemporary aesthetic. In particular, they worked hand-in-hand with the architect to ensure their indoor-outdoor kitchen rose to their expectations. Washed in white, the expanse of marble flooring features soft veining to maintain an organic aesthetic that would meld with the view through the two walls of floor-to-ceiling glass. One of these glass "walls" opens up the space to the outdoors.

The indoor-outdoor kitchen features sleek white cabinetry, a suite of stainless-steel appliances, and an island with a sink. The work area is set at the far back of the room, leaving the majority of the floor open to all possibilities. This versatility was important to the couple, allowing them to use the room for a variety of activities. In the end, modern life met mother nature in a stylish, serene design.«

SPECIAL FEATURES
Modern aesthetic, two walls of floor-to-ceiling windows, indoor-outdoor room that opens on side, marble flooring with soft veining, fully equipped kitchen setup

PRODUCTS USED
Cabinetry: Sleek white ultra-modern cabinets
Flooring: Marble with soft veining
Hardware: Brushed nickel
Lighting: Recessed can lighting; natural light, thanks to two walls of floor-to-ceiling windows

PHOTOGRAPHER: PHOTOBANK

Florida Hot-Spot

WHEN HOT FLORIDA DAYS transform into temperate nights, the last thing any homeowner wants to do is to be stuck inside. However, with "staycations" being the latest trend, simply setting out a lawn chair will no longer make the cut.

These Gulf-area homeowners were amazed by the amount of yard available after they cleared away the wild brush that had been allowed to overrun the lawn of their newly purchased house. Seizing the opportunity to reinvent the property, they installed this grilling space, complete with a tucked-away waterfall to enhance the already-tropical feel of their surroundings. Backlit at night, the sound of running water adds an aura of peace and serenity. The lighting of the waterfall, combined with small yard lights and candles, softly illuminates evening dinners and parties.

Adding to the tranquility is the richness of the dark-granite countertops and the sheer efficiency of the stainless-steel grill, complete with a burner and a ventilating grill hood. Set against the backdrop of a cobblestone wall, the cooking area is secluded and intimate. With everything built in and tucked away, the sharp clean lines of the space are able to shine. Large-tile flooring ties the yard together, connecting the cooking area to the waterfall behind. A stainless-steel KitchenAid rolling dumbwaiter serves both form and function when entertaining.

With everything they need for a relaxing getaway right in their own backyard, these homeowners won't be going anywhere soon.«

SPECIAL FEATURES
Backlit stone waterfall; stainless-steel grill and hood; dark-granite countertops; large-tile floors; intricate stone-wall divide, creating a separate kitchen space

PRODUCTS USED
Flooring: Oversized tile
Countertops: Dark granite
Grill: KitchenAid stainless steel with burner and grill hood
Lighting: Backlit stone waterfall, small yard lights

PHOTOGRAPHER: KITCHENAID

SELECTING APPLIANCES

WHEN IT COMES TO FOOD PREPARATION, what's more fun than cooking outdoors? Friends and family gathered together, enjoying flavorful food, makes grilling, in a word, great.

Our love affair with backyard cooking took off in the early 1950s when George Stephen, a Chicago welder, created the Weber Kettle, a domed charcoal grill. It allowed folks in the Windy City to cook over even heat, without generating too much smoke. A decade later, Illinois' Walter Koziol, whose company manufactured gas lamps, invented the gas grill.

Today, the grill remains the focal point of most outdoor kitchens. Eight out of every ten households in the United States own a grill. And, of course, today it's a big business with seemingly limitless options, from the simple tabletop hibachi to a high-end infrared grill that is the centerpiece of a complete outdoor kitchen.

Choosing the right grill for your outdoor kitchen can be overwhelming. This chapter will help make the task a little less daunting. You'll also get a look at other appliances and accessories, including ovens and refrigerators, that will help you make your outdoor kitchen complete.

This outdoor kitchen has it all. It includes a grill, a warming drawer, an extra burner, a refrigerator, an ice machine, and a bar center—and a breathtaking view.

Choosing a Grill

The grill is the heart of your outdoor kitchen—and it may end up being its most expensive component, too—so choosing the best one is an important decision. Grills come in all shapes and sizes. Before you invest your hard-earned money, make your decisions about the following:

GRILL TYPES

Will your outdoor kitchen feature a built-in grill or one that stands on its own? A grill that's built into a countertop or grill island usually has more cooking capacity and plenty of work area on each side. A free-standing unit on wheels, on the other hand, is better if you want to be able to move your grill, either to clear the area when you're not cooking or to move the grill to a more optimal position when the weather or season changes.

FUEL OPTIONS

Gas—natural gas or liquid propane (LP)—is by far the most popular choice here. For flavor, however, many traditionalists won't go near a gas grill, instead favoring a charcoal unit. Electric and pellet grills are other options. (For more on making the proper fuel choice, see "The Fuel Types" on page 168.)

SIZE

This refers to the size of the cooking surface. To determine how big your grill should be, think about how you plan to use it. Are you a weekend griller who will be cooking for your small family? If that's the case, a grill with a surface area of 300 to 450 square inches should suffice. A bigger family might require a grill with 450 to 600 square inches of cooking area. If you plan to host large neighborhood parties, invest in a grill with a cooking area that's at least 600 square inches. The types of food you cook are important when determining grill size as well. Rib roasts and shish kabobs take up a lot of space. Burgers and hot dogs are more compact.

Freestanding grills, such as this 623-sq.-in. model with fold-down side shelves, come fully assembled.

BTU

A Btu (British thermal unit) is a standard measure of energy, but it isn't a true measure of a grill's cooking power or heat output. A Btu rating is a measurement of the heat produced by the grill per hour. More important than a high Btu rating is the ability of a grill to reach and sustain desired cooking temperatures—and this depends on a number of factors, including size and heat distribution. A large grill with what seems like an impressive Btu rating may not perform well if the ratio of Btu to area is inadequate. In general, grills with two burners should produce 30,000 to 50,000 Btu, or about 100 Btu per square inch of cooking surface. Burners should be designed to distribute heat evenly to all areas of the cooking surface.

CONSTRUCTION

Look for a durable unit. You don't want a model that rattles when you shake it. Most of the top grills today have bodies made of heavy-duty cast aluminum or stainless steel. If you're going with a freestanding unit, make sure the wheels roll easily—and that they lock.

This built-in gas grill is wide—53 in.—but it still fits snugly into one end of this compact outdoor kitchen.

You'll likely have pay more for a solid, sturdy grill, but with proper care it should last many years.

ASSEMBLY

How easy is it to put your grill together and get it ready for outdoor entertaining? Most folks don't want to bring a new unit home and find out it takes an engineering degree to understand the novel-length owner's manual. Take some time in the store to get an idea of what prep work is required. The best brands reduce the amount of assembly required. Look over the manual to see whether it's going to be easy to follow or not.

ACCESSORIES

Some people prefer the bare-bones approach, while others want every accessory known to man. Most will fall somewhere in between. Figure out what you want out of your grill, and then determine which "extra" is a must. Perhaps a built-in rotisserie has to be included. Maybe you can't do without a removable smoker box. The grill of your choice doesn't have to come pre-packaged with every accessory you may want. (To get an idea of what accessories can be added later, see pages 170 and 171.)

SERVICE

If a part breaks, will it be easy to replace? If you need troubleshooting help, is a toll-free hotline available 24/7?

WARRANTY

You're going to invest hundreds of dollars—maybe even thousands—in your grill, so you want to know you're covered should something go wrong. Most major manufacturers stand behind their products; many offer warranties that cover parts and labor for one to five years and burners for a lifetime.

Grill Features

If your repertoire is limited to burgers and hot dogs, there is no need to go all-out for a top-of-the-line unit. If you're an avid griller, however, you'll want to consider a unit with superior features. Here are some:

IGNITERS

Many gas grills are ignited with a knob or a push button. The knobs give off two or three sparks per turn, while buttons give off one spark with each push. The best—and most reliable—choice is a battery-powered electronic igniter, which produces continuous sparks as long as the button is held down.

BURNERS

Burners are the workhorses of the grill, providing the gas and flames. Most grills come with steel burners, although some are stainless-steel, cast-iron, and cast-brass units. The latter three tend to last longer because they are not subject to rust. Look for a grill with more than one burner; having only one burner may result in hot and cold spots on the cooking surface.

INFRARED BURNERS

Want a higher, more intense heat? If so, you'll want to consider a grill with infrared burners or invest in a stand-alone infrared burner. (Some gas grills combine infrared and standard burners in one unit.) Unlike traditional burners, infrared burners do not require a secondary heat element, such as ceramic briquettes, which means less heat will be lost. Infrared burners concentrate the flames through a ceramic tile that has thousands of microscopic holes. This process converts the fuel into infrared energy. The intense heat—and the lack of a secondary heat element to trap drippings—keeps flare-ups to a minimum.

GRATES

Don't overlook grates—these important components are it's where meat meets fire! Grates should be strong and sturdy, provide good heat transfer, and have a nonstick surface. Most gas grills have stainless-steel, cast-iron, porcelain-coated cast iron, or porcelain-coated steel grates. Stainless steel provides even heat distribution and will work well for a long time, but it will not hold the heat as well as cast iron. Cast iron requires more maintenance; you need to keep it cleaned and well oiled to avoid rusting. Porcelain-coated grates are rustproof and easy to clean, but they can chip.

RADIANTS

Sometimes referred to as heat diffusers, radiants, which are located between the burner and the grate, distribute heat evenly and vaporize drippings. The most common radiant is lava rock. Lava rock is irregularly shaped and doesn't hold heat evenly. It's also porous, which allows grease to build up. When not changed regularly, flare-ups are possible. Pumice stone is similar to lava rock but is less porous, resulting in fewer flare-ups. Ceramic briquettes cost more than lava rock and pumice stone but distribute heat more evenly and are self-cleaning. Long-lasting metal bars provide even heating and the fewest flare-ups, because food drippings are vaporized as they contact the hot plate.

DRIP TRAYS

Excess drippings must be properly channeled away from the burners to avoid flare-ups or, even worse, a

Infrared burners are ready to grill in a matter of minutes and cook twice as fast as a standard burner.

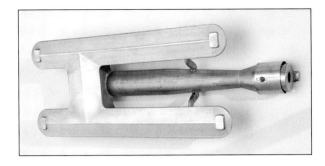

Burners, such as the "E" burner, left, need to be replaced more often than most grill parts, so look for ones with warranties for 10 years or more.

Grates with closely spaced bars, below, make it less likely that food will fall through them. These grates are made of heavy-duty stainless steel.

grease fire. A good drip tray covers the entire cooking area, won't stick or catch when opened and closed, and should be accessible from the front of the grill. The deeper the tray, the less often it needs to be emptied and cleaned. If you plan on purchasing a charcoal grill, be sure it includes a removable ash-collection tray for easy cleanup.

SHELVES

Many freestanding grills include exterior shelves that flip up (usually from the side) or are fixed, offering additional space for food prep. These shelves are usually made of plastic, but some are cast aluminum or stainless steel.

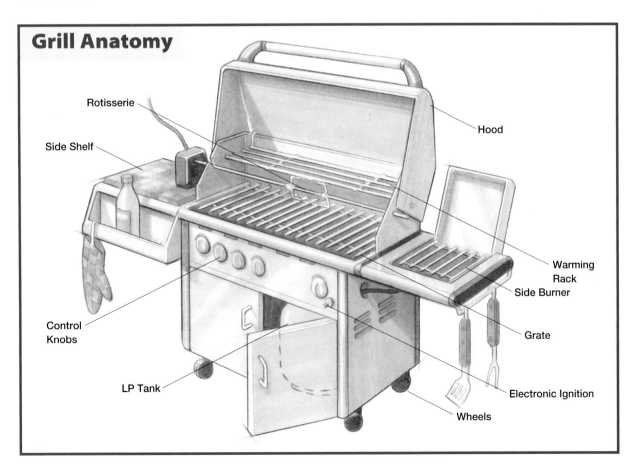

Grill Anatomy

Rotisserie

Side Shelf

Hood

Control
Knobs

Warming
Rack

Side Burner

Grate

LP Tank

Electronic Ignition

Wheels

Grill Price Categories

You get what you pay for. That's the general rule of thumb when you buy almost anything, including a grill. Here's what to expect when you're grill shopping. Note: these are general guidelines, not hard-and-fast rules.

BASIC

The basic grill, ideal for serving four to six people, has a small grilling area with one burner (maybe two) that has one control. Most of these no-frills grills have enameled-steel housing, with plated-steel or chrome-plated aluminum cooking grates. You'll be hard-pressed to find any stainless-steel parts or accessories in this category. Most basic grills cost $100 to $300.

This midrange grill, above, has three stainless-steel burners, a 12,000-Btu side burner, porcelain-enameled cast-iron grates, and a painted-steel frame.

This basic grill, left, offers 308 sq. in. of surface area, two burners, and porcelain-coated grates.

This high-end grill, opposite, is a freestanding unit with stainless-steel grates. It includes three 22,500-Btu burners, two 15,000-Btu side burners, and a 14,500-Btu infrared burner.

MIDRANGE

This is the best choice for most people. The grilling area is larger and includes two or more separate burners, which allows greater control of heat. The burners are backed by longer warranties (often 10 years or more). Most midrange grills have a cast-aluminum or stainless-steel housing, though the stainless steel may be of the 400 series, which has less corrosion-fighting chromium than the 300 series. The premium grates are often coated with porcelain enamel. The majority of grills in this category include electronic ignition, a side shelf, and perhaps a rotisserie or a smoker tray, but not many more extras. Most midrange grills cost $300 to $600.

HIGH-END

The top-of-the-line grills have more burners (often five or six) that provide more heat. The burners have a lifetime warranty, and often an infrared burner is included in place of a traditional burner. The housing is 300-series stainless steel.

The grates may be, too, though some are cast iron. Grills in this category come standard with all sorts of accessories—side burners, smoker trays, rotisseries, and storage compartments, among others. High-end grills, which are often stylish and aesthetically pleasing, will last a lifetime. And they should, considering they can cost anywhere from $600 to $5,000 or more.

SMART TIP

WHEN TO BUY

Don't wait until a week before your big Fourth-of-July party to go grill shopping. Head to your local home-improvement center or specialty retailer—or check out some retail sources on the Internet—at the end of the outdoor cooking season to get the best deals, especially on grills with extra features.

The Fuel Types

Food may be the fuel you need to power your body, but you won't get food from an outdoor kitchen until you decide what kind of fuel-powered grill to buy. Gas grills are the most popular, followed by charcoal units, and pellet grills may be the wave of the future. Electric grills are also an option.

This charcoal grill uses a gas assist to light the coal fast, combining the tradition of charcoal with the ease of gas.

GAS

The numbers don't lie. Gas grills are by far the most popular grill type. According to the Hearth, Patio & Barbecue Association, 71 percent of grills owned in the United States are of the gas variety. Gas grills offer push-button ignition, quick preheating, and a steady heat supply that is controlled with the simple turn of a knob. There are no fires to stoke or ashes to empty.

A gas grill is simply a grill that uses gas from a tank or a natural-gas line for fuel. The grills are fueled by liquid propane or natural gas—not both. Some manufacturers offer conversion kits, but there is no easy way to convert your grill from one fuel type to another. Be sure to select a grill that accepts your fuel source. Liquid propane is typically stored in cylindrical tanks and is almost always located on a shelf below or hung on a bracket beside the grill. You can expect to get 20 to 30 hours of use from a full tank. Natural gas-fueled grills do not require tanks, so the possibility of running out of gas during cooking is eliminated. They are permanently hooked up to your home's natural gas supply. Excluding installation costs, natural gas is about half the cost of propane to operate.

CHARCOAL

A charcoal grill is basically a receptacle for coals with a cooking grate above it. The principle fuel is either natural lump charcoal or charcoal briquettes (compacted ground charcoal, coal dust, and starch). Natural lump charcoal burns hotter, which means you use less. Briquettes produce more consistent heat, but many people feel charcoal imparts a better flavor. Ah, flavor. That's the reason many people own charcoal grills. These units, which are generally the least expensive, are the choice for purists who want to barbecue (a long, slow heating process), not grill (cook quickly, directly over high heat). The coals—and the smoke they create—provide flavor that many barbecue enthusiasts swear by.

Charcoal grills have come a long way since the hibachi dominated the market 30 years ago. Today you can find anything from a hibachi to a kettle grill (a round or nearly round unit with a domed lid that typically stands on three legs) to a large, powder-coated steel model. Built-in charcoal grills are not as readily available as their gas counterparts, but the number keeps rising.

PELLET

You may not have heard of pellet grills yet. If gas prices continue to surge, you will. Small wood pellets provide the fuel and infuse food with flavor from the smoke. The pellets, stored in a hopper, are available in a variety of flavors, including mesquite, hickory, apple, and alder. (The latter is great for fish.) They can be fed into the firebox at vari-

GAS VERSUS CHARCOAL

Here are some of the basic pros and cons of gas and charcoal grills. Take a look, and then decide which grill fills the bill.

Gas Grills
- Easier to turn on
- Heat up in about 10 minutes
- Have a steady heat supply
- Provide even heat
- Offer greater temperature control
- Produce great-tasting food
- Generally more expensive
- Straightforward food prep
- Relatively easy to clean and maintain

Charcoal Grills
- No push-button ignition
- Heat up in about 20 minutes
- Coals must be replenished
- Burn hotter
- Not as easy to control temperature
- Produce great-tasting food with distinctive flavor
- Generally less expensive
- Thrill of cooking with a fire
- More cleanup involved

An LP tank, above left, even when it's empty, weighs as much as 18 to 20 lbs. This full-extension drawer makes it easy to replace the tank when it runs out of gas.

Pellet grills, left, are safe—there are no gas leaks or smoldering briquettes to cause worry. This model automatically supplies wood pellets to accurately provide three different cooking temperatures.

able rates—slower for barbecuing food, faster for grilling. Pellet grills are increasing in popularity thanks to their energy efficiency and their clean-burning properties. The grills—and the wood pellets—are not widely available yet, so they tend to be the most-expensive grill choice.

ELECTRIC

Electric grills make up only a tiny fraction of the barbecue market, and they can be more difficult to find than the other types of grills, but they may be worth a look. Electric grills, available as built-in or freestanding units, are easy to operate and maintain. They are also ready to cook in the shortest amount of time. An electric grill is often smaller than its gas and charcoal counterparts, so it may be more suited for those living in an apartment or a condominium. But even then it may not be the best choice. Many argue that the flavor an electric grill imparts doesn't come close to what a charcoal or gas model produces.

Grill Accessories

You've selected a grill. That's the first step. Now it's time to outfit your grill. What you get will depend on your budget and your cooking style. If you want to turn your grill into a multifunctional cooking center, consider the following items:

SIDE BURNER

If you plan on preparing an entire meal outdoors, a side burner is a must. It allows you to boil a pot of water for corn or lobster, heat sauces, or stir-fry vegetables, eliminating the need to run back inside again and again. Look for one with two burners in a single unit with a continuous grate, which will allow you to use large pots and pans.

WARMING RACK

Temperature drops considerably as the distance between the cooking surface and the burner increases. A warming rack is simply a shelf, often removable, located above the main cooking surface that keeps food warm. Many warming racks can be adjusted to two or three different levels, depending on the model.

ROTISSERIE

For slow, even cooking, consider buying a rotisserie. This is a motorized spit (a long metal rod) that suspends and slowly rotates food over the grate. The rotisserie is a popular grill attachment because it slowly roasts, creating foods crispy on the outside and tender and juicy on the inside. The more weight the rotisserie can handle, the better—the best can accommodate at least 40 to 50 pounds. Keep in mind that a rotisserie requires an electrical outlet for the spit motor.

PIZZA STONE

Pizza stones sit directly on the cooking grate, using the grill's high heat to produce pizzas with crisp crusts. The stone holds heat and helps create a simplified version of an Italian brick oven. Pizza stones work great for flatbreads and calzones, too.

SMOKER BOX

These perforated metal containers hold wood chips and give a smoky flavor to your food. Also known as smoker trays, smoker boxes are positioned on a gas grill's lava rocks or ceramic briquettes, or on a charcoal grill's grate. Removable smoker boxes are included with most high-end grills, but some are built in as part of the cooking grate. Wood chips come in all sorts of flavors, from apple and maple to mesquite and pecan.

WOK RING

A wok is a bowl-shape utensil used for stir-frying vegetables, shrimp, or pieces of meat to create Asian-inspired dishes. A wok ring is a stainless-steel ring that positions the wok properly on a regular burner. So this accessory is ideal for stir-fry fans.

GRIDDLE

Set a nonstick cast-iron griddle on the grate to cook the perfect pancakes or crepes. Some griddles are two-sided; they cook the pancakes and crepes on the smooth side and use the grooved side for preparing bacon or sausage.

GRILL BASKET

A grill basket is a must-have item if you want to grill whole fish, veggies, and other fragile foods. A hinged wire basket with a latch allows you to  flip the food with no mess, making searing your favorite filet incredibly easy.

VEGETABLE RACK

Use a vegetable rack to keep food such as potatoes and corn away from direct contact with the grill.

THERMOMETER

If your grill doesn't come with a built-in thermometer (often hood-mounted), you may want to consider one. A thermometer,  which is most useful if you are smoking or slow-cooking food, will provide approximate grilling temperatures and help control the heat more precisely. To be sure your meat is cooked at just the right temperature, however, the gauge needs to provide specific, accurate information. Remote-control models have a receiving unit that you can carry around with you—it will beep when the food is done.

TOOL SET

No matter what you're cooking, it's necessary to have the right tools  on hand. Any utensil set for grilling should include a spatula, fork, tongs, knife, basting brush, and grill-cleaning tool. Stainless-steel tools with long, durable handles are recommended.

RANGE HOOD

Ventilation must be considered, especially if your outdoor kitchen is attached to the house or is under some sort of shelter. Range hoods,  also known as vent hoods, remove the smoke and grease that cooking generates, making the kitchen cleaner, safer, and more comfortable. A range hood can be mounted to the wall or ceiling, depending on the configuration of your outdoor kitchen. It's important to get one that is big enough to capture the rising cooking vapors. The best models have heat sensors that automatically increase power if temperatures reach a certain level.

LIGHTING

Grilling at night? Be sure you have light. Your outdoor kitchen should be well lit, but if you need additional light near the grill, consider a stand-alone fixture with a rotating head or a light that can clamp onto the grill handle or a nearby object. On some high-end grills, halogen lights are built into the grill hood.

GRILL COVER

Many manufacturers provide a cover when you buy your grill. A good grill cover should be constructed of heavy-duty vinyl with a nylon lining to protect your grill from the elements. You don't want your cover getting blown off on a windy day, so get one with Velcro tabs, snap closures, zippers, or a drawstring to ensure a snug fit.

When it comes to outfitting your grill, remember that you don't need every accessory. It's okay to "rough it" a little outdoors and leave the perfectly prepared meals to inside dining. Instead of relying on a rotisserie, for example, have a guest tend to the chicken. Sometimes, the simplest solutions are the best ones.

Other Cooking Options

A grill isn't the only way to go when it comes to preparing meals in an outdoor kitchen. Sure, it's the best bet if you want cheeseburgers or chicken breasts, but perhaps you're interested in smoking a few racks of ribs. Or maybe you'd like to bake pepperoni pizzas with crunchy crusts. The adventurous souls may like to barbecue some *picanha* (a special cut of beef popular in Brazil). If any of these scenarios make your mouth water, you should think about the following cooking options:

SMOKERS

Tell some folks you are going to "barbecue" something on your grill and they'll give you a strange look. To many people, a true barbecue consists of slowly smoking meat at a low temperature. Grilling is cooking directly over a high heat, charring the meat's surface and sealing in the juices, while barbecuing refers to using an indirect, low heat for a longer period of time to smoke-cook the meat. If the latter interests you, you may want a smoker.

The main difference between a charcoal grill and a smoker is that a smoker keeps the fire away from the food. Water smokers, which are shaped like a bullet, include a heat source on the bottom, grilling racks on the top, and a pan of water in between, creating

a type of indirect cooking. The water pan ensures that foods will stay moist even after hours of cooking. Wood chips rest atop a heat source—charcoal is the most popular—and flavor the food. A dry smoker is the more traditional of the two types of smokers. It has an offset firebox on one side and a cooking chamber on the other. Rather than using charcoal or gas, dry smokers burn small pieces of wood in the firebox. A vent on the side opposite the firebox draws heat and smoke from the fire across the cooking chamber. The cooking chamber fills with smoke, giving the food its characteristic smoked flavor. Cooking times for a dry smoker tend to be longer than those for a water smoker because the food is farther from the heat source.

KAMADOS

The egg-shaped Kamado, a thick-walled ceramic cooker, is great for smoking at lower temperatures—between 150 and 250 degrees F—for long periods of time using only a small amount of charcoal. The ceramic walls retain the heat, and vents at the top and bottom allow you to control the temperature. Cooking space is limited; the largest models have a diameter of about 24 inches. Get one as large as possible because the long cooking times essentially make preparing everything at once a must.

PIZZA OVENS

For the ultimate outdoor dining experience, many people are putting in a wood-fired pizza oven. These ovens, which reach temperatures unattainable in an indoor oven—600 to 700 degrees F is common—produce intense, even heat, resulting in pizzas with crisp crusts and sizzling toppings. It takes an hour or two for the oven to reach the required temperature, but

A dry smoker, left, contains the fire and keeps the temperature low. Cooking low and slow produces tender pieces of meat that practically fall off the bone.

The centerpiece of many new outdoor kitchens is a wood-fired pizza oven. This refractory concrete pizza oven, right, is heavy, so it requires a concrete footing.

the pizza cooks in a matter of minutes. The ovens can also be used for baking breads, roasting vegetables, and cooking meat.

Pizza oven kits, which cost about $2,000, are designed to be easy to install. Generally, the kit is housed in a masonry structure that can safely contain the high level of heat. The insert may be made of porous clay or concrete combined with firebricks, and the structure is usually covered with stucco, stone, or tile.

ADOBE OVENS

An adobe oven is a low-tech alternative to a pizza oven that will keep more cash in your wallet. The basic adobe oven is simply an enclosure made of hardened mud, with a deep, arch-shaped opening in the front and a vent hole in the back. Many adobe ovens are sculpted works of art that look like something out of *Star Wars*. Adobe ovens, popular in the Southwest United States and Mexico, are not very heavy and do not require concrete footings, but they should rest on a fire-safe surface.

CHURRASCO BARBECUES

A *churrascaria* is a Brazilian or Portuguese restaurant where large quantities of meat are prepared in a barbecue with a rotisserie that supports two or more levels of spits. This style of cooking is referred to as "churrasco." Now, you can create these same pieces in your outdoor kitchen. A churrasco barbecue cooks meat using wood charcoal or firewood.

The firebox portion of this churrasco barbecue is the perfect place to cook chicken, beef, and sausage on spits.

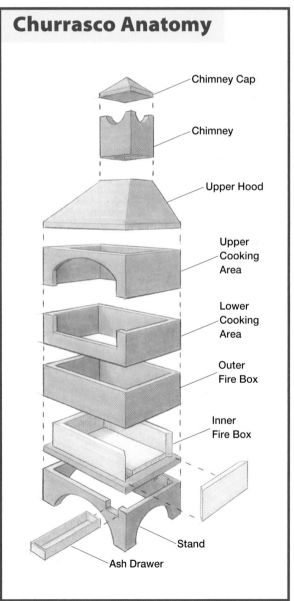

Churrasco Anatomy

- Chimney Cap
- Chimney
- Upper Hood
- Upper Cooking Area
- Lower Cooking Area
- Outer Fire Box
- Inner Fire Box
- Stand
- Ash Drawer

The 24-in.-wide fridge holds the drinks, and the 15-in.-wide ice machine provides a steady supply of ice cubes.

Refrigerators

You've got the meat. What about the cheese, the condiments, and the drinks? It doesn't make much sense to cook outdoors if you have to keep running back in the house for items. Add a refrigerator, and your outdoor cooking area nearly becomes a fully functioning kitchen.

Under-counter refrigerators are the choice for most outdoor kitchens because they're out of sight; they're protected from the elements; and they allow counter space above. A full-size refrigerator should only be considered in a large, fully protected kitchen in a warm climate. Many manufacturers now make refrigerators for outdoor use. You will pay more money, but you'll get a fridge that typically has a larger compressor to keep your food cold and includes wiring and electronics designed to withstand the elements. The best ones are made of stainless steel, which stands up to the most extreme environments. Make sure your

refrigerator has heavy door hinges that create a good door seal. It should also be front-vented so it can be placed under a countertop.

If you last purchased a compact fridge back when you were an undergrad living in a cramped dorm, be prepared to spend a bit more money this time. Most outdoor kitchen refrigerators start at $1,500, and a 24-inch stainless-steel model could set you back more than $2,000. Of course, you could always go low tech and just fill a cooler with ice and drinks and haul it outside. Put it on a stand or low shelf for convenience.

SMART TIP

SAVE ENERGY

To reduce the amount of energy your refrigerator uses, keep it out of direct sunlight and position it away from the grill or any other heat source.

Other Outdoor Appliances

If you want your outdoor kitchen to be as efficient as its indoor counterpart, it makes sense to include some amenities. Small appliances are as indispensable outside as they are inside. Be sure that any appliance you will use outdoors is manufactured for that purpose. Whenever possible, look for items with the UL (Underwriters Laboratories Inc.) seal of approval.

WARMING DRAWER

A warming drawer that has a thermostatic temperature control will keep finished food items warm until dinner is served. The variable moisture control will help maintain the proper food texture, whether it's moist or crisp or somewhere in between. You'll often need to keep a lot of items—everything from bread to beets to beef—warm at the same time, so look for a unit with deep drawers.

ICE MAKER

An ice maker, a slim appliance that can fit into a tight under-the-counter spot, will require a water line. Some models may also require a drain. If you're going to entertain often, look for a model that makes a large amount—25 to 35 pounds—in a short amount of time. Compact ice maker-refrigerator combos also are available.

WINE COOLER

What complements a fine meal better than a nice glass of wine? A wine cooler with an adjustable thermostat keeps your bottles at the perfect tempera- tures. Many wine coolers include automatic settings for red or white wine. Buy a wine cooler with a security lock if you're worried about anyone raiding your collection. The smallest units hold 12 to 24 bottles; the next in line accommodate 28 to 32. The best come with canted shelves to keep corks moist.

BEER-KEG DISPENSER

This is perhaps the final touch to your outdoor kitchen. A typical dispenser for the outdoor kitchen holds half kegs and quarter kegs. What better way to keep beer cold, fresh, and ready to serve? Some models include shelves that allow you to convert the dispenser into a fridge.

Let's not forget about the simple plug-in appliances. As long as you keep them sheltered, you can equip your outdoor kitchen with a blender, coffeemaker, toaster oven, waffle maker, juicer, and whatever else you may need. With so much available to outfit your outdoor kitchen, the only limitation is your imagination. Visit a few Web sites on the Internet to check out some of the latest outdoor kitchen appliances.

A dispenser that holds a half-barrel keg keeps the beer cold and saves valuable refrigerator space.

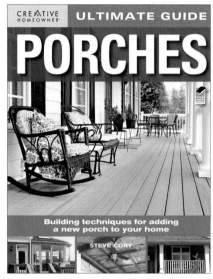

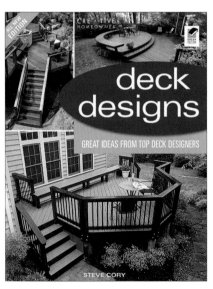
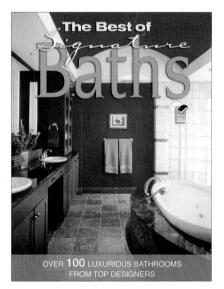